REMEMBERING

DILLON county

SOUTH CAROLINA

REMEMBERING DILLON COUNTY SOUTH CAROLINA

CARLEY WIGGINS

THE History PRESS

Published by The History Press
Charleston, SC 29403
www.historypress.net

Cover image: Dillon County Courthouse. *Courtesy of Judge J.E. Lockemy*.

First published 2008
Second printing 2015

Manufactured in the United States

ISBN 978.1.59629.575.9

Library of Congress Cataloging-in-Publication Data

Wiggins, Carley.
Remembering Dillon County, South Carolina / Carley Wiggins.
p. cm.
ISBN 978-1-59629-575-9
1. Dillon County (S.C.)--History--Anecdotes. 2. Dillon County (S.C.)--Biography--Anecdotes. I. Title.
F277.D5W54 2008
975.7'85--dc22
2008033422

This book is dedicated to my wife, Helen Lane Wiggins who came into my life six years ago and convinced me that I had qualities and talents that I never even considered. It is only through her encouragement, patience, and understanding has this book been made possible.

For all the many hours that she has spent in research, taking of pictures, interviewing people and correcting my mistakes, I dedicate Remembering Dillon County, South Carolina.

CONTENTS

THE JAMES K. BRABOY STORY

Teaching is a profession that I have always had a great deal of respect for. I have known a lot of teachers in my life. Some I thought were very dedicated to their jobs in seeking to educate and train their students to the best of their abilities. Then I have known some that I felt were just in it for a paycheck and the benefits that the job offered. As I think back to my school days, and all the teachers I studied under, only two stand out in my mind as being really dedicated to giving their best to the profession they had chosen. I started school in 1946 at a small country school called Dothan, which was about six miles from Dillon and eight miles from Latta in Dillon County. There were six grades at the school—grades one through three were in one room and four through six in another room.

My first teacher was Mrs. Kate Berry, and she was one of the two that affected my life the most. Teaching was not as accelerated as it is now; you were taught a basic education of reading, writing and arithmetic. Even though Mrs. Berry taught three grades, she always took time to explain what she was trying to get across to the students. She always took the time to work with students that needed extra help. Mrs. Berry always looked after the smaller kids on the school ground, to make sure the older kids didn't take advantage of them. Since I didn't have brothers or sisters in school, this meant a lot to me.

After my first year at Dothan, the school closed, and I was sent to Latta. This was a big deal for me; the school was much larger and we had hot lunches and indoor bathrooms. I was elated when I found out that Mrs. Berry had also been moved to Latta and that she would be my second-grade teacher. I think that the leadership she gave me in my first two years of school gave me a big head start that would last me through my formal education.

The second teacher I would like to mention was Miss Hettie Willoughby. I wrote an article about her a couple of years back, and so many people who knew her commented on the article. Most agreed she was a great teacher.

Miss Hettie was a person that you either loved or hated—there was no in-between. She had one purpose in life, and that was to be sure you got some math in the time you spent in her class. Miss Hettie was what you would call "an old maid school teacher" because she never married and teaching school was her whole life. I had her for math in the fifth and sixth grades, and in Miss Hettie's class you behaved or you felt her wrath.

Miss. Hettie could not teach school today, because she had complete control of her classroom. You paid attention or you would get to know her famous paddle. She would probably be arrested today for child abuse, but she didn't really have to paddle that many students, because you knew she could and would if need be. In her class, you learned more than math. You learned strict discipline, which in my opinion we need more of today.

This story is about a teacher that I never knew or had the opportunity to talk to, even though he taught school in Dillon County for thirty-seven years. I read a little about him in the local newspaper back in the late sixties, when he won the Teacher of the Year award for the state of South Carolina, but I never met the man or took time to find out something about him. There were never any books published about him, or anything on television, so I figured he must not have been too special.

When I began writing newspaper articles about five years ago, I was always looking for new and unusual stories to write about, and for some reason, the name of James K. Braboy kept running through my head. All I knew was that he taught school at some obscure school called Leland Grove. Even though I have lived in Dillon County all my life, I had no idea where this school was. When I married my present wife in 2002, she lived about six miles from the school, and I began to ask her some questions about the school and Mr. Braboy. She didn't know a lot about the man personally, except that she had seen him on occasion and that he was an Indian. She stated that he was always very nice, and had a good manner about him.

In August 2005, I decided that I was going to research this man and maybe write an article on him. Bear in mind that this man had been deceased for twenty-nine years, so I figured that information might be pretty hard to find. One of the first places I went to was the Dillon School District office to talk with the superintendent of personnel. I asked to see the file on Leland Grove School, and she answered "Well, they didn't keep many records back then." She showed me the Leland Grove folder, and to my amazement, there were four sheets of paper in the folder. Leland Grove operated for forty years or perhaps longer, and the only records they had were four sheets of paper.

The superintendent said to me, "Carley, that school has been closed for more than thirty-five years; I wasn't even here when Leland Grove closed." It sounded to me like that they might have been a little ashamed of this school. I found out later that there was plenty of information on the white schools that had been closed for years. The next day, my wife and I went to the library to get what we could from the old newspapers that were on microfilm. There were just a few articles about James Braboy and Leland Grove, and they were all during the time that he was South Carolina Teacher of the Year. I knew nothing about James Braboy's life or his time at Leland Grove.

I was determined to uncover this story, and the best place to start was with the people that knew him and went to Leland Grove School. So began a journey that would take us many miles and many hours of interviewing people in both North and South Carolina. A great breakthrough came when we found Mr. Braboy's son-in-law, through the reading of Mr. Braboy's obituary. His name is Cecil Madden, and he lives in Charlotte. We got in touch with Mr. Madden, and he was delighted that we were going to do the story. He visited us a couple of times and shared many pictures, articles and stories that Mr. Braboy had saved over the years. Mr. Madden's wife, Dorothy Louise Braboy Madden, had passed away just a few months before we got in contact with him. Cecil Madden helped more than words can say to make this story come about. Mr. Madden had nothing but the highest respect for his father-in-law.

The James K. Braboy story would take more research and time than anything I have written, but to tell this exceptional man's story was worth it all. What I planned to be one newspaper article turned out to be nine weeks' worth of articles .When I decided to write this book, there wasn't any doubt that this would be my feature story. With respect to an extraordinary man, this is the James K. Braboy story.

James Knox Braboy was born October 6, 1906, in Pembroke, Robeson County, North Carolina, on a tobacco farm, the oldest son of Tecumseh Bryan and Mary Jacobs Brayboy. (You will notice the difference in the spelling of the name, the reason to be explained later.) James Braboy had thirteen brothers and sisters. When his mother died in 1929, his father married Ruth Carter and they had five children. There was also an adopted child, for a total of twenty children. The Brayboy family was Indian, probably of Cherokee descent, but now known as the Lumbee tribe.

The Lumbee tribe is the largest Indian tribe east of the Mississippi, with a population of over fifty thousand. The tribe has also become the most educated tribe in the country, through the very fine University of North Carolina–Pembroke campus. The heaviest concentration of Lumbees is in Scotland, Robeson and Bladen Counties of North Carolina. The Brayboy

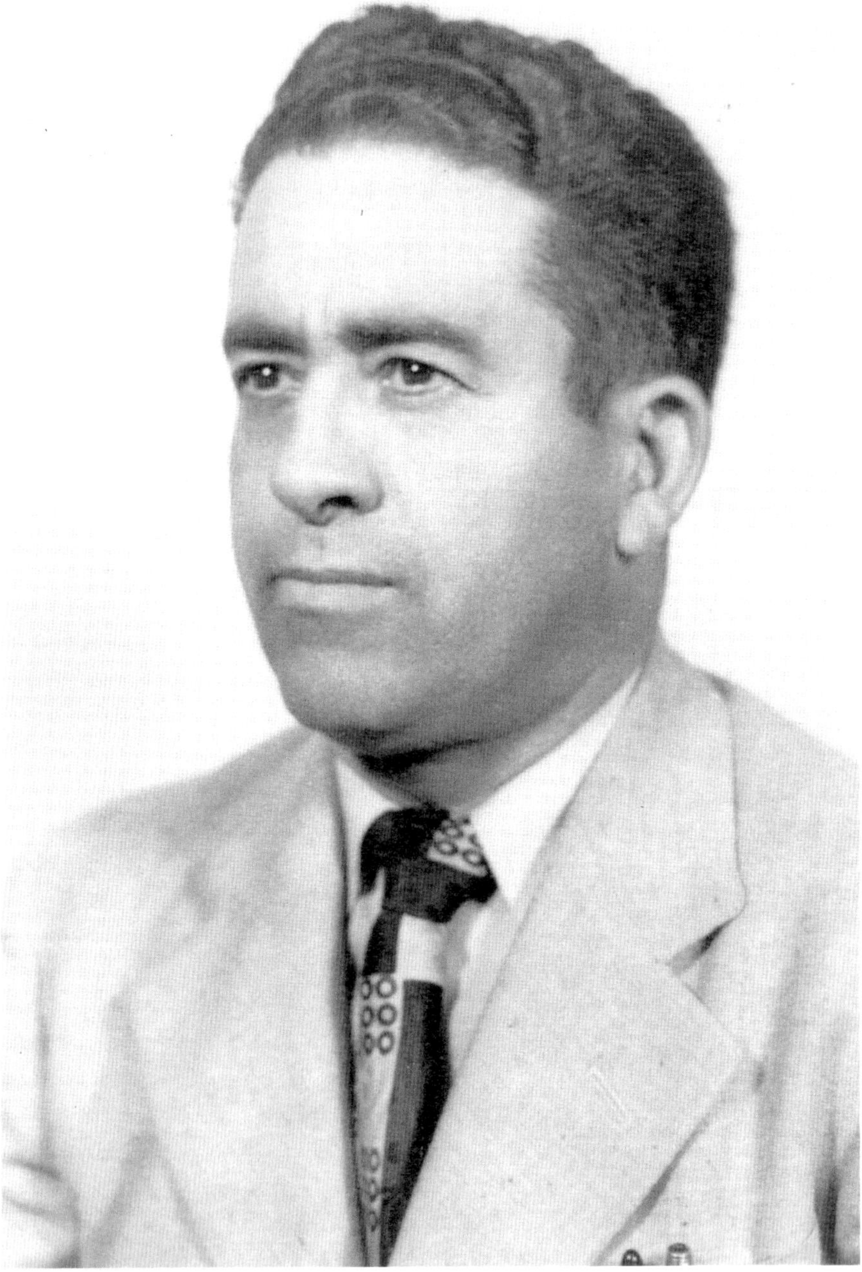

James K. Braboy in his younger years. *Courtesy of Cecil Madden.*

name has been changed down through the years; it began as Brave Boy, which came from their Indian ancestors. James Braboy is the only one I can find that used his spelling of the name. I think this was due to the circumstances under which he left the state of North Carolina. You might say that James Braboy was born with a strike against him; he was born an Indian and there were not many opportunities for him in that time. He worked on the tobacco farm as a youth, and his father also had a sawmill. With all those children, Mr. Brayboy had plenty of help to run his business.

Baseball was a big part of James Braboy's young life. He loved the game and played with Indian teams around Pembroke. James also loved school, and his passion as a young boy was to be a school teacher. He graduated high school at Pembroke and enrolled at the Indian Normal School, which would later become Pembroke College. A two-year diploma was all that the school offered, but he could teach school at that time on the two-year certificate.

James Braboy started his teaching career at the Indian elementary school near Pembroke. He was offered a teaching position in Nash County, North Carolina, due to a large movement of the Indians to that county to work on the tobacco farms of Nash County. His stay in Nash County didn't last very long, as the Indians had a dispute with the landowners and moved back to Robeson County. Braboy also came back and took up teaching at Pembroke once again.

On December 19, 1931, James Braboy married Lily Costin Hall from McColl, South Carolina. There was only one problem with this marriage: Lily Hall was a white woman, and in those times it was against the law for an Indian to marry a white woman in Robeson County. Word got out about the marriage, and soon James Braboy was arrested and brought before a judge. The judge ordered him to leave his wife or leave the county.

Forced to leave Robeson County, the young couple moved across the North Carolina line to McColl, South Carolina, but there was no place for James to teach school. Things were much different here because there were no Indian schools. The couple wound up in Dillon County, and James Braboy began to do the only other thing he knew, and that was to farm. With a plow that someone in Dillon gave him and a rented mule, Braboy began to sharecrop a farm near where Old Pee Dee Park is located. James Braboy was at the lowest point in his life. He had studied so hard to become a teacher, and now he was living in poverty because of the color of his skin. James admitted later that he hated farming, but what was he to do? There were no other jobs he could get. The couple lived in a two-room sharecropper's shack, the kind of home in which they would spend much of their life.

Faith had always been a big part of Braboys' life. He was a religious person from an early age, and each day, he prayed to God to send him a better life.

One night, as he was praying, a knock came at the door. When he opened the door, two men were standing there. Braboy asked what they wanted, and one man answered, "We have come to bring you some fish." The young man said they couldn't afford to buy any fish, but the man said, "They are a gift, and we have a matter to discuss with you." The two men were Riley Dial, an Indian, and Floyd Branch.

The men said they were from the Carolina Community of Dillon County, which is in the northeast part of Dillon County near the North Carolina border. Both of these men were landowners in that area and they explained that they had a problem. It seems that over a period of time, about five hundred Indian people had migrated over the North Carolina border and settled in the Carolina Community to work on the farms, and the problem was that they had children who had no place to attend school. They said there was a one-room building that the county said could be used as a school for the Indian children. James Braboy stood in amazement as they told their story. This was truly an answer to his prayers. Little did he know the long hard road that would be his life for the next thirty-five years.

James K. Braboy moved his wife and infant daughter, Dorothy Louise, to the Carolina Community of Dillon County in 1934 to teach at the Leland Grove School. The school at that time was just a shabby, one-room building in perhaps the poorest section of the county. The house they would move into wasn't any better than the school—just a sharecropper's shack with two or three rooms. There was no running water or indoor bathrooms at the school or the house. This would be one of three houses that the Braboys would live in while in the Carolina Community.

The Carolina Community is located fourteen miles from Dillon in the northeast part of Dillon County, very near the North Carolina border. The area is covered with pine forests and sandy land, which is hard to grow a decent crop on. At that time, most of the area was owned by several large landowners, who lived in nice homes while the Indians and poor whites lived in the sharecropper houses that were furnished by the owners. Only a few Indians owned their own farms: Luke Hunt, who had raised a large family, owned a small farm, and Riley Dial, who was related to Hunt, had his own farm.

The Little Pee Dee River runs through the middle of the Carolina Community, which accounts for a lot of the sandy soil in the area. Leland Grove School was located near the river at a place called McInnis Bridge. Attorney Jack McInnis said that his father, John D. McInnis, taught at Leland Grove during the Depression, and that he was paid in script because there

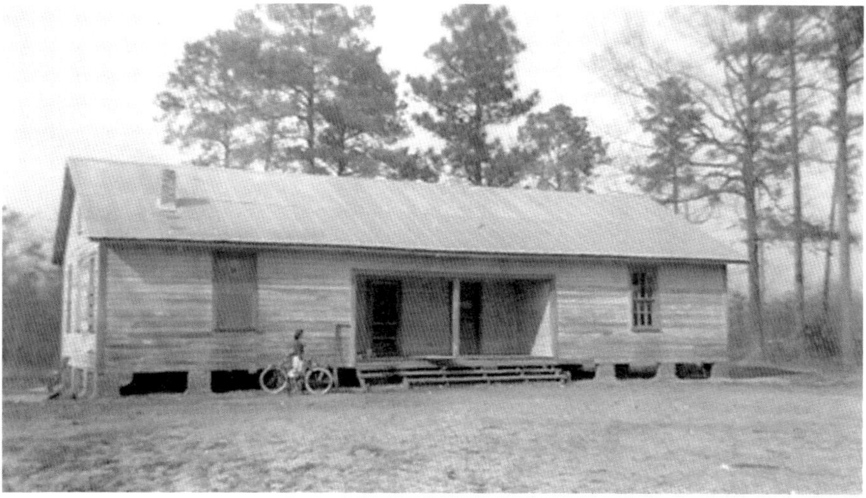

Leland Grove School as it appeared in 1934. *Courtesy of Cecil Madden.*

was so little money at that time. He said that his father would trade the script to the bank for a portion of what the script was worth.

When James Braboy opened the school for classes in the fall of 1934, he realized he was in for a real challenge, but at least he would be teaching school, a job he felt he was called for. Many of the students would miss the first few weeks of school because they would have to work on the farms. Dorothy Hunt Neilson, who was a student at Leland Grove when Mr. Braboy arrived, shared a lot of facts with us about the school in those days. The roads were dirt, the bridges were made of wood and a lot of the students would have to walk several miles to school. Mr. Braboy would meet the children at the bridge and walk across with them to protect them from falling in the water. There were no buses at that time, and Mrs. Neilson told us that at times it would be nearly dark when they arrived back home from school.

There was no electricity and no running water inside or outside the school—not even a hand pump. Water was carried to the school from a spring near the river. She said that it really did not bother the students, because they were poor and this was about all they had at home. The building was heated with a "Warm Morning pot-bellied heater" that was fueled with wood that Mr. Braboy and the larger boys would cut from the woods. She stated that he was such a good man, and today she still has fond memories of Mr. Braboy and how he treated all the students the same, never showing any differences among them. Mrs. Neilson has lived in California for the past forty years and is in her mid-seventies. She still has relatives in the area and comes back to visit about once a year.

The early years at Leland Grove were the worst for James Braboy, mainly due to the lack of teaching material. One student told us that she remembered when the school didn't even have a dictionary. When Mr. Braboy approached the school district for help with books, he was told that these kids didn't need very many books because they were stupid anyway. This was the kind of discrimination that James Braboy faced for many years before federal funds, when each community supported their own schools. Since Leland Grove was in a poor community, there was very little funding for the school.

There were seven grades at the Leland Grove School when Mr. Braboy arrived, and he taught all seven grades in the beginning. His main emphasis was to teach these children to read and write and to add and subtract in order to keep them from being completely illiterate when they left the school. He knew that when they left Leland Grove that it would probably be all the education they would have, since they were not wanted in the white schools. James Braboy was teacher, principal, custodian and later the bus driver. He *was* Leland Grove School to the fifty students that he taught.

Mrs. Macie Barfield lives in the community and is the oldest member of the Pee Dee tribe at the age of ninety-two. The Pee Dee Indian tribe is a small tribe that has been reorganized in the last thirty years, with members

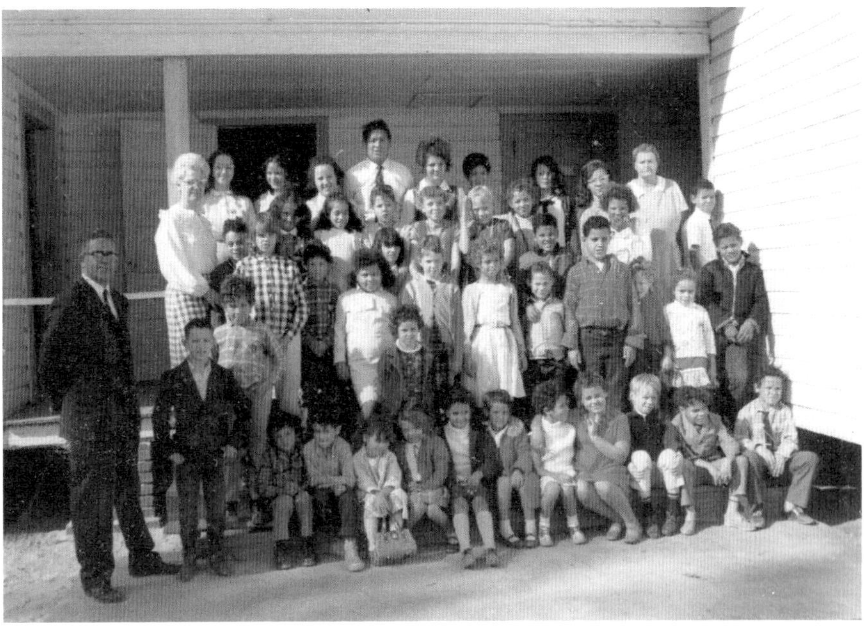

Student body at Leland Grove School. *Courtesy of Cecil Madden.*

mostly in Dillon and Marlboro Counties. The tribe was thought to have vanished for two hundred years. Mrs. Barfield remembered James Braboy well; she said that he would hold bake sales, put on plays and hold auctions in order to put money into the school so it could stay open.

We talked with Ernest Barfield, the son of Macie Barfield. Ernest is seventy and was a student of Braboy's. He had such good memories of Mr. Braboy. He talked about helping him work on the old bus when the school finally got one and bringing in wood and coal to stoke the heater that warmed the school. Ernest showed us a folder of perfect attendance records that he received at Leland Grove, and he was as proud of these as a person might be of a college degree. He had them laminated to protect them all these years. Mr. Barfield did not graduate high school; the education he received at the school was all he ever got, but he worked at a textile plant for years, and he declared that he would not have been able to fill out an employment application had it not been for James Braboy.

Every school has a star pupil, I guess, and Leland Grove had English Jones. English Jones was there in the early days of Mr. Braboy. If I have my years correct, he would have been about ten years old when Braboy came to the school. Jones was just the son of a dirt-poor farmer like all the other students, and he missed a lot of school due to helping on the farm, but Mr. Braboy saw something in English Jones that some of the other students didn't have: the ability to learn well and learn quickly. In the fall of 1937, school had started back, but there was no English Jones. That afternoon, as he was walking home from school, Braboy saw Jones over in the field, picking cotton.

English Jones was about to have the most important conversation of his life as the teacher walked over to him. Mr. Braboy asked, "Son, why are you not in school?" Jones replied, "Well sir, I have to help get the crop in, and I am already behind in school, so I probably won't go back." Braboy talked to the boy for a while, and then decided to talk to the boy's father. He went up to the boy's house where his father, Pete Jones, was standing in the yard. Braboy asked, "Mr. Jones, why won't you let English come back to school?" Pete Jones turned to Braboy and said, "What does he need to go to school for; he can read and write, that's more than I can do." Mr. Braboy pleaded with the man to give the boy a chance for an education. After some time, Jones said, "I'll tell you what, I'll send him back to your school, but you will see, he's nothing but a poor Indian boy and that's all he will ever be!"

English Jones went back to Leland Grove and put every possible minute he could into his schoolwork. The boy completed the seventh grade at Leland Grove and his mother passed away shortly after. The father sent him to

Pembroke to live with relatives. Jones enrolled in the schools at Pembroke and graduated Pembroke High School at the age of twenty-one. He was three years older than most of his classmates. Soon after high school, Jones joined the army and served his country well. When his duty was completed, he wound up in the state of Kentucky and enrolled at the University of Kentucky.

English Jones worked and lived in a boiler room at the college and got a four-year BS degree. By now you might think that Jones had accomplished everything he wanted in life, but he came back to the state of North Carolina and received his master's degree from North Carolina State. From there, he went to Wake Forest and got his LLD, and finally back to Pembroke College for his doctorate. English Jones had worked at every kind of job imaginable and lived under some bad circumstances to become Dr. English Jones.

English Jones didn't stop there. In 1962, he became the first Indian president of Pembroke College. The school had 758 students when he became president and had mostly been an Indian school from its beginning. The doors were just beginning to crack for non-Indian students, and Jones carefully led the school through the integration days. In 1972, Pembroke State College became the University of North Carolina at Pembroke. Jones became the first Indian chancellor to ever become the head of a North Carolina university. At that time, the school had an enrollment of 2,334. Today, the enrollment is over 6,000 and is one of the fastest-growing schools in the country.

Dr. Jones never forgot where he came from. He said on many occasions that if it had not been for Mr. Braboy, he would still be in that cotton field. English Jones would come back to the country school many times to visit his old friend. When Mr. Braboy received his Teacher of the Year award in 1970, English Jones was there. When James Braboy passed away in 1976, English Jones was there, and it was said that he wept openly at the loss of his mentor. James Braboy and English Jones had common bonds: they were both Native Americans, and they had seen the worst the world had to offer.

English Jones married Margaret Sheppard, and they raised a good family: two sons and a daughter. Jones, like Braboy, was a man of faith. He was very active in his church, Harper's Ferry Baptist Church, where he served as a deacon and taught Sunday school for twenty-seven years. In 1979, Dr. Jones retired from the university due to a health condition. Two years later, in 1981, he lost a bout with cancer; English Jones died at the age of sixty. He had overcome tremendous odds in his life to achieve the things that he did, but there is a lot to be said for the country teacher that saw something special in this man.

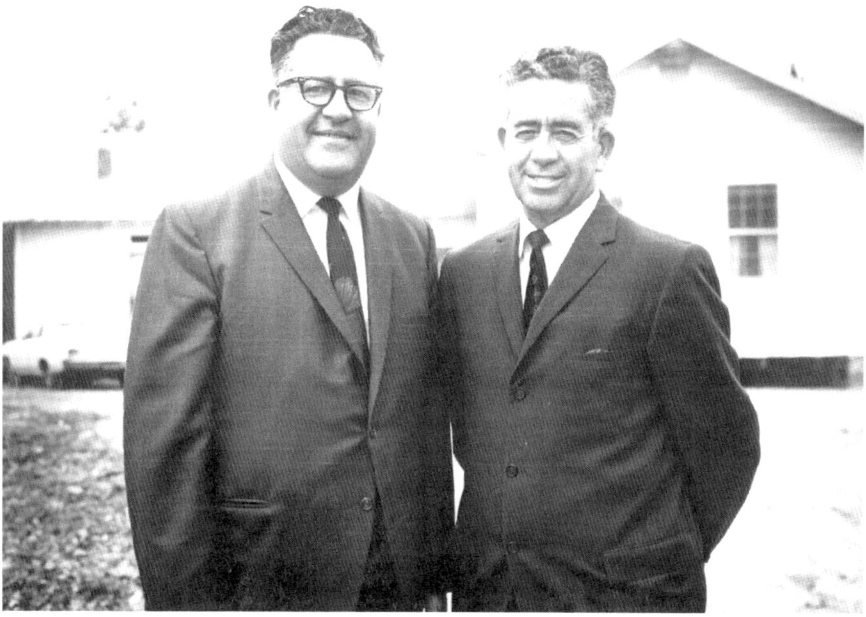

James K. Braboy (right) with his star student, Dr. English Jones. *Courtesy of Cecil Madden.*

Slowly, things began to improve at Leland Grove School. By 1940, the school had added a second room, and another teacher was hired to help Braboy. Sallie Brooks came from North Carolina to teach grades one through three. Mrs. Brooks was also of Indian descent; she boarded with a family near the school and went home on the weekends. In the early forties, the school got electricity for the first time, but it was still a far cry from the white schools in the county. To my knowledge, the school did not have running water until the 1960s—an indoor hand pump was installed in later years. Also in the early forties, the school got an old bus and James Braboy took on another job as bus driver. I have not been able to find out how much money James Braboy made at the school, but it is my belief that he only received a teacher's salary. One of the many other things he sacrificed for the children.

Brothers Bernice and Ed Hunt, now in their seventies, were students at Leland Grove, and they talked at length about Mr. Braboy. To these two men he was a hero, a mentor and a father figure. Ed told me about the day he got into a fight on the school ground. Mr. Braboy called him inside and gave him a talking to. Mr. Braboy did not use corporal punishment unless absolutely

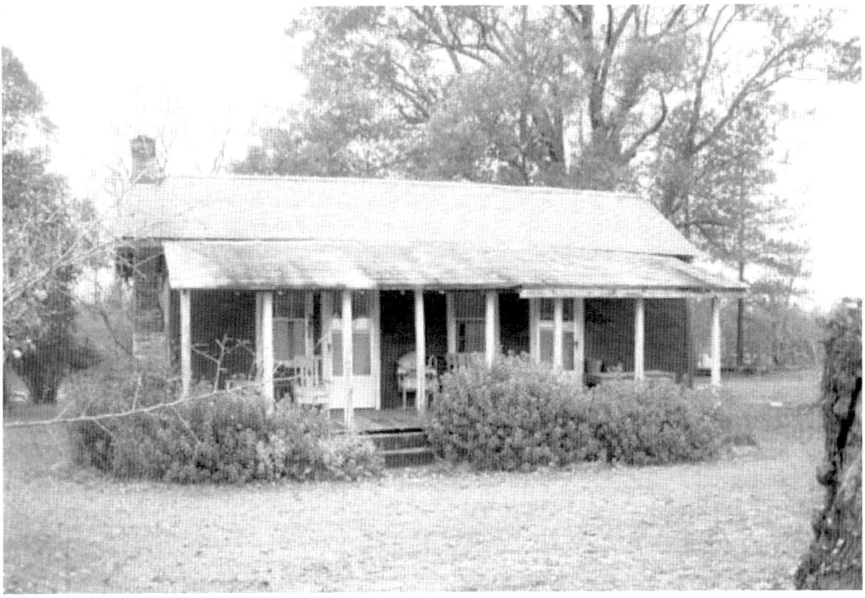

One of the homes that James K. Braboy lived in during his years at Leland Grove School. *Photo by Helen Wiggins.*

necessary, but Ed said he would rather have a whipping anytime than for Mr. Braboy to give him a lecture. Randy Hunt, a son of Ed Hunt and a successful contractor in Laurinburg, North Carolina, said that he didn't attend Leland Grove, but the Braboy name was a household word in their home when he was growing up, and he was glad to see Mr. Braboy get some recognition.

In 1949, Mr. Braboy's only child, Dorothy Louise, had finished the seventh grade at Leland Grove, and he had to find a place for her to continue her education. They had lived in three houses while in the Carolina Community and none of them had running water or indoor bathrooms. He moved his family to McColl, South Carolina, some eighteen miles from Leland Grove, to yet another small house on Church Street without any modern conveniences. Years later, he added two more rooms and a bath. He was not allowed to drive the bus to McColl, so he had to leave the bus at another location and commute to his home, but fortunately by then he had been able to buy a car.

Dorothy Louise Braboy reported to the all-white school in McColl, and when she was signing up for classes, the clerk asked what race she was. When Dorothy said, "I am Indian," the clerk answered, "Nonsense, there are no Indians in South Carolina." Dorothy insisted that she was an Indian. Her father had always instilled in her a pride for her Native American heritage. The clerk sent her to class, but she said that Dorothy could not be counted present until she admitted she was white. There were other dark-skinned people in the school who probably had Indian blood as well, but they didn't claim to be Indian, so there was no problem with them. Dorothy Braboy went to the school for a week and was counted absent each day until she told the told the school officials that she was white.

Time moved on, and the year was 1952. Segregation still ran very deep in the rural South. Things had improved a little at Leland Grove, but it was still a school for Indian people only, and most of the citizens of Dillon County didn't know it existed. Mrs. Bessie Norton became school food supervisor for Dillon Schools in 1952, a job she would hold for thirty years. I have known Mrs. Norton for years. She is now in her nineties, and I have always found her to be a very warm and caring lady.

Mrs. Norton said on her first trip to Leland Grove, she was completely astounded by these beautiful Indian children. She said there were about fifty at the school, and most were shabbily dressed, but they were clean and mannerly. As Mr. Braboy showed her the school, which was still only two rooms, some of the smaller children tried to hide behind the larger students. These children saw very few people outside of their own community. The school did not have a cafeteria as yet, but a cook had been hired part time to prepare lunch for the children. The cook was Mrs. Lizzie Chavis Locklear, and to my knowledge, she had no formal education, but she was said to be a very good cook. The menu at Leland Grove was mostly vegetables from Mr. Braboy's garden and what the parents would donate, along with the funds they got from the district. The food was cooked and taken to the students' desks by some of the older girls. Mrs. Locklear had grandchildren who attended the school while she worked there. She worked at Leland Grove until the school closed in 1970. When the school finally closed, Mrs. Norton talked her into working several years at Maple Junior High school.

Mrs. Norton went to work immediately to get some help for the school. She talked to Joe Martin, who was superintendent of the Dillon schools, and they were able to get some equipment from one of the white schools that had been closed. The school got its first refrigerator and first electric stove. When the stove was delivered, Mrs. Locklear said, "I don't know if I can cook on that thing." She had never used an electric stove. Mrs. Norton also got the school's food budget increased; she stated that Mr. Braboy would request a lot of dried beans. When she told him that he didn't have to feed those children dried beans every day, he replied, "But Mrs. Norton, they love those beans so much." They were not used to eating the finest of foods. Mrs. Norton said that Mr. Braboy was perhaps one of the most courteous and polite men she had ever met in her entire life.

I mentioned in the beginning that Mr. Braboy was a religious man, and when he moved to the Carolina Community, he joined Fairview United Methodist, located about a mile from the Leland Grove School. The Fairview church was founded in 1912 and always had a mostly Indian congregation. Archie Hunt and Riley Dial cut the timber and hand-hewed the lumber to make the shingles and sills for the church. D.F. Lowery was the first pastor of the church. The church still operates today, still with a mostly Native American congregation of about fifty members. We talked to several people who said that James Braboy was as faithful to his church as he was to his school. Reverend Robert Magnum was pastor of the church for a few years and told about how Mr. Braboy was the "backbone" of that church. He was an inspiration to all those who attended. He was a deacon, served on the board of trustees and taught the adult Sunday school class for over twenty years. Reverend Magnum said that in the sixties, the church began to show some growth, but the church was without funds to build additional space, so they pulled some old school buses behind the church and held Sunday school in them. Ann Cummings remembered attending Sunday school in one of the buses.

While researching the Braboy story, we visited with Mr. L.S. "Lila" McColl and his wife Violet McInnis McColl, who are prominent farmers and landowners in the Carolina Community. Mr. McColl came here from Marlboro County in 1942 and bought a small farm, which has multiplied several times since, and now they have three sons active in the farming business. Mr. and Mrs. McColl talked about the Indian people who lived in the area and mentioned several families that lived on their farm for years. Both agreed they were hardworking, honest people and had been an asset to their farming interests.

The McColls both knew James Braboy well, especially Mrs. McColl, who taught at Leland Grove in the school year 1969–70, the last year that the school operated. They said that Mr. Braboy had been a credit to their community for the work that he had done with the Indian people of the surrounding area. John McColl, the youngest son of the McColl family, had substituted for Mr. Braboy as a bus driver from time to time. Mrs. McColl shared a story with us about the year that she taught at Leland Grove. By this time, Mr. Braboy had begun to get some recognition for his work at the school, and Mr. Alan Schafer, founder and owner of the tourist complex South of the Border, invited all from the Leland Grove School for a Thanksgiving meal at South of the Border. Mr. Schafer treated everyone to a fine turkey dinner with all the trimmings. Mrs. McColl stated that some of the students were a little reluctant to eat because they didn't know what they were eating. For many of them, it was their first time eating in a restaurant.

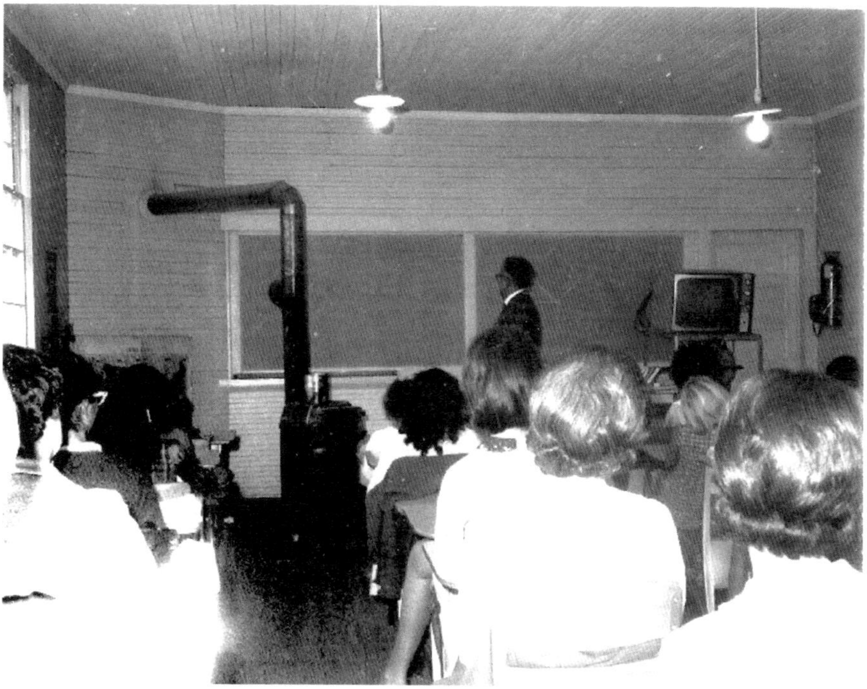

James Braboy teaches night school for adults at Leland Grove School. *Courtesy of Cecil Madden.*

Teachers that taught with Mr. Braboy came and went at Leland Grove; the conditions at the school were not very good, so most did not stay very long. I mentioned Sallie Brooks, who was the first; others that I know about were Charles Luther Moore, Tom Oxendine, Annie Hammonds, Ludula Wilkins, Frances Locklear Kerns and Violet McInnis McColl, who taught the last year the school was open. All but two were Indians.

The town of McColl, where James Braboy lived from 1949 until his death in 1976, has a nice little museum for a town of its size. The museum is well stocked with memorabilia from years ago that has been donated from McColl and the surrounding area. Mr. Grady Hubbard is the curator, and this man at the age of eighty-five has a fantastic knowledge of McColl. We went to see the museum one day, and I was very impressed with the rooms of old relics, including many items that even I had no idea what they were, and a huge collection of pictures of all the mayors and other notable people who lived in and around McColl. After he showed us through, I asked Mr. Hubbard, "Did you know a man named James Braboy?" He thought for a minute and said, "Yes, I believe I did know him. He lived on Church Street." I asked if he knew about Mr. Braboy being the Teacher of the Year in South

Carolina and also one of the top five in the nation. Again he hesitated, "Why yes, I do remember something about that." I answered back, "Then why is there nothing in this museum about the man?" Mr. Hubbard dropped his head and said softly, "I really don't know." As we started to the car, I knew too well why there was nothing about Braboy in the museum; it was because he was an Indian and lived on the poor side of town.

Shelby Chavis attended Leland Grove from 1952 until 1959. When she finished the seventh grade, at the insistence of her mother and especially Mr. Braboy, she entered the eighth grade in Dillon. Shelby graduated high school at Dillon in 1965, but she said that those were five of the worst years of her life. She was one of just a handful of Indians in the white school, and she said she was picked on every day. She stated that she was called "Croatan" more times than she could count. Croatan is the name of an Indian tribe from long ago, but it was used as a negative word for Indians just as the n-word is used for blacks. Shelby stuck it out and got her diploma, but many would drop out after a few weeks or months because they just couldn't stand the ridicule.

I have not been able to find how many went on to make a better life for themselves from the school, but I will mention some that I know about. Sherman Brooks, son of teacher Sallie Brooks, went on to be a professor at one of the large universities; Joseph Hunt got a college degree and became a teacher in Georgia; Elizabeth "Lib" Owens became a nurse and works at Southeastern General Hospital in Lumberton, North Carolina; and Vanessa Barfield McIntyre is head nurse at Dillon Family Medicine in Dillon. Some made it out of the Carolina Community, but many still live there and will spend the rest of their days in run-down mobile homes, despite all the encouragement that Mr. Braboy could give.

After the newspaper articles began to come out about the Leland Grove School, I ran into Mrs. Osborne "Betty" Wallace at the Post Office. Betty told me she was the first speech therapist at the Dillon School District, and that Mr. Braboy wanted her to go to Leland Grove and test some of his students that he suspected might have a speech problem. She said she went to the school, and the only private place to test the students was in the shade under a tree. She remembered how concerned he was about the children.

When I started working on the Braboy story, some said I would not be able to get much out of those Indian people, but as we began to visit and talk about Mr. Braboy, they just opened up like a faucet. We interviewed dozens of people and could not find one who had a negative word to say about James K. Braboy.

The year was 1958, and James Braboy had been teaching elementary school for almost thirty years with a two-year diploma from Pembroke College, which was all that was required at that time. Times had changed and now it was mandatory that a teacher have a four-year degree. Mr. Braboy had been taking summer classes at Pembroke when time and money would allow. He worked hard to get the necessary credits for the degree required in order to continue teaching. That summer, James Braboy graduated with honors from Pembroke College with a four-year degree in elementary education. He was fifty-two years old when he received a BS degree.

The 1960s were the best years that James Braboy would spend at Leland Grove School. Federal funds had become available for the schools, and Leland Grove was finally getting some of the things that they had needed for so long. A third room was added to the school, and now the children had a small cafeteria, and Mrs. Lizzie Locklear had a larger place to prepare the meals. A small library was added, and the students had access to more books than ever before. The school had a better bus, one that could be depended on without breaking down so much.

One of the most amazing things I found out about was when the school got its first telephone in 1968. Southern Bell's John Brooks got the surprise of his life when he went to the school to introduce his company's tele-trainer program. This program was devised to train third-grade students how to use a telephone properly, Brooks explained, "but this was the first time I've had children who have never used a phone at all." In grades one through three, there were seventeen children who had not even had a phone in their hands; only one student had a phone in their home. Braboy pointed proudly to the progress of his little school. "Running water, a movie projector, a small library, educational TV, and now a telephone," he mused. "And maybe next year, I can get a bus driver, and I can retire from that job." I think Mr. Braboy knew that integration was on his doorstep, but he hoped to be able to keep the school open for the sake of the Indian children.

The school year of 1969–70 was certainly the highlight of James Braboy's career as a teacher, but it would also be perhaps the saddest year for him, as he found out early in the year that Leland Grove would close after that school year. Integration was fully in place, and the schools were now racially mixed. The state would no longer fund a school just because it was an Indian school. Leland Grove would be one of the last small schools to close in the state and certainly the last Indian school to operate in South Carolina. Superintendent H.E. Corley had been over the Dillon schools for some time now, and was perhaps the first head of the schools to look past Mr. Braboy's skin color, recognizing him for the job he had done for the past thirty-four years and seeing the qualities that this dedicated man possessed.

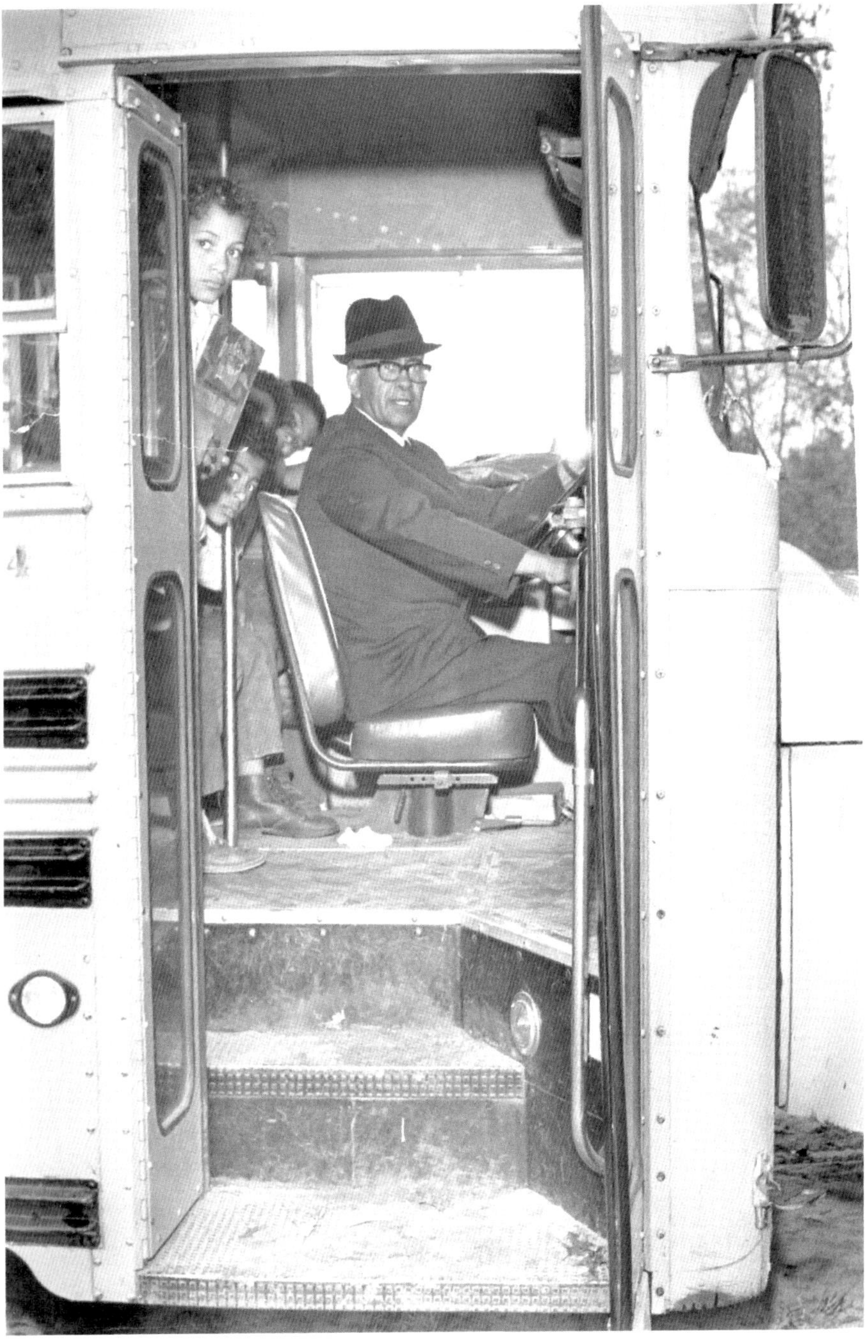

James K. Braboy, the school bus driver. *Courtesy of Cecil Madden.*

James K. Braboy was nominated as Teacher of the Year for Dillon School District and was unanimously elected. By this time, most of the teachers in the district had realized just what this man had done for the people of his community and readily cast each vote for him. From there, Mr. Braboy went to the state finals and again won by a landslide as South Carolina's Teacher of the Year for 1970. He was the first man to receive this award and the only Lumbee Indian ever to be Teacher of the Year. A huge reception was held at Dillon High School for Mr. Braboy, and over a thousand people came to give their congratulations to a man that had dedicated thirty-five years of his life to the task of educating people of his race. Many local and state dignitaries were on hand to pay tribute to this modest teacher. State Superintendent of Education Cyril Busbee said, "It looks like everybody in his community is here as well as his neighbors from McColl." Mr. Braboy's eyes were glistening as he accepted congratulations from each one. He stated at the reception, "I just can't believe that this is happening to me."

Look magazine sponsored the National Teacher of the Year Awards in San Francisco that year, and James Braboy was selected to compete in the national competition. I doubt seriously that Mr. Braboy had ever been out of the two Carolinas, but he proudly went to represent the Palmetto State in the nationals. Braboy was in some heavy competition in San Francisco;

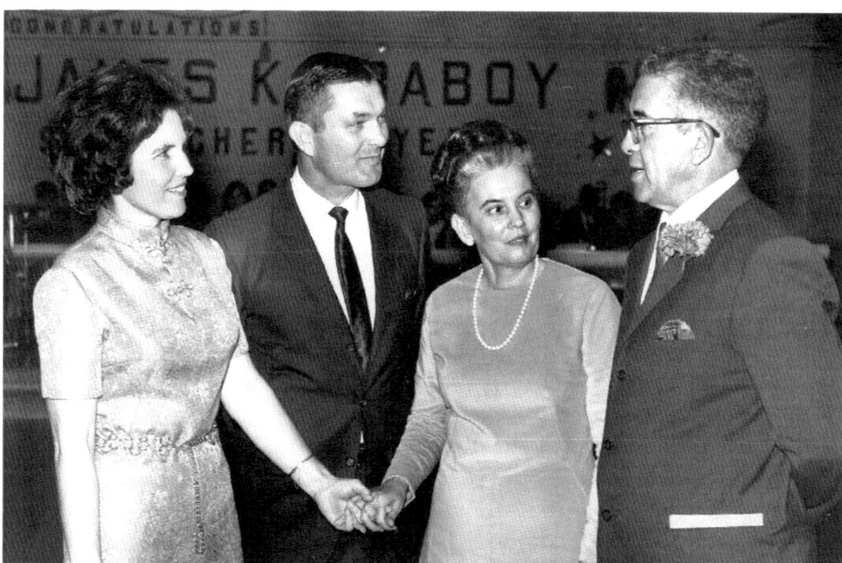

Vivien Reed (former Teacher of the Year), Superintendent H.E. Corley, Elizabeth Hendrix and James K. Braboy, South Carolina Teacher of the Year 1969–70. *Courtesy of Cecil Madden.*

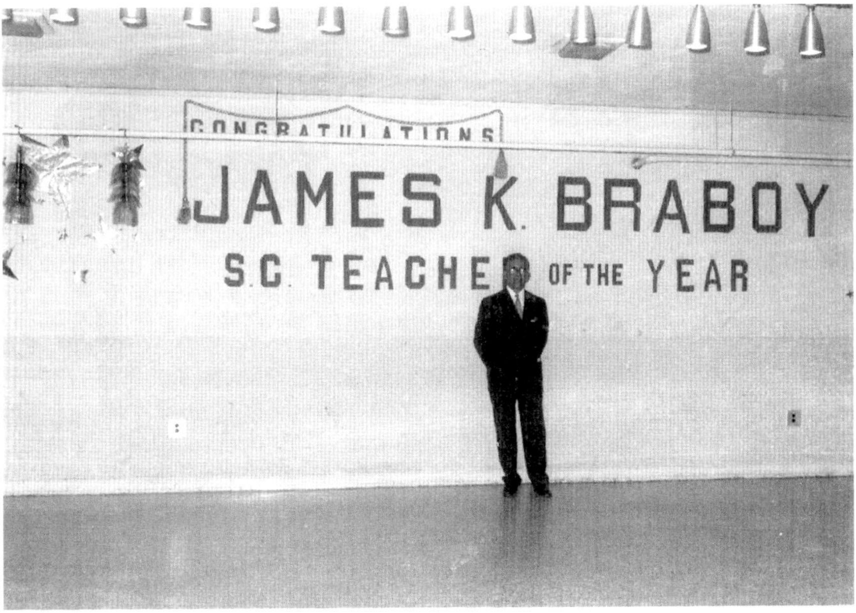

The 1969–70 Teacher of the Year awards ceremony. *Courtesy of Cecil Madden.*

he was up against teachers with strings of degrees and accomplishments that would amaze anybody. Braboy finished in the top five in the entire nation. These five had their pictures and a written tribute printed in the very popular magazine. This was said about James Braboy in *Look* magazine:

> *James Knox Braboy, a Lumbee Indian, teaches grades four to seven, Leland Grove School, Dillon, South Carolina, is principal-custodian-bus driver, adult educator and apostle of perseverance (B.S. at 52). "K" Braboy, grandfather of three, rates a doctorate in dedication for his 42 year war on ignorance and poverty in the Carolinas.*

James Braboy was sixty-three when he became South Carolina's Teacher of the Year. After being in the limelight for the first time in his life, Braboy settled back down at Leland Grove School and prepared for the inevitable, the last day of school, when he would lock the doors on the little country school where he had spent the last thirty five years for the last time. He hated to see the school close, but at least he knew his students would be with people of all races now. He also pondered his future and wondered if he was ready to give up working in a job that he loved so much. The Dillon School District had offered him a job as co-principal of the elementary school in Little Rock, which would remain open for several more years. He had told the superintendent that he would let him know his answer by the end of the school year.

In the fall of 1970, James Braboy reported to his new job at the Little Rock elementary school as co-principal. The other principal was Ulysses Madison, a black man who, like Mr. Braboy, spent his entire adult life in the field of education. The two had known each other for many years, and they made a good team at Little Rock. Mr. Madison is retired now and lives just outside of Dillon. We talked at length with Mr. Madison about his time with Mr. Braboy. Madison said that Mr. Braboy was a little behind the times from his slow-paced method of teaching at Leland Grove, but what he lacked in training he made up for in the ability to work with both teachers and students. He said that everybody liked Mr. Braboy; he never lost his temper or shouted at anyone, and he was just a man that always had self-control over everything he did. At break time, instead of staying inside, Mr. Braboy would go outside and be with the students. Just as he did at Leland Grove, he would take time to umpire a baseball game for the kids.

The school at Little Rock was like a different world for Mr. Braboy. The building was a nice brick structure with spacious rooms, indoor bathrooms and a nice cafeteria and there was a teacher for each class. He also had something he had never had before: his own private office. Mrs. Winnie Stanton, who is now in her eighties, was Mr. Braboy's secretary. Mrs. Stanton could not say enough good things about her former boss. She talked about his good nature and noted that he was the most courteous man she had ever met. She remembered how he would bring fresh vegetables from his garden to share with the entire faculty. Things went well for Mr. Braboy in his first year at the new school, and he was very proud that a good number of the students were Indians from the Carolina Community.

As Mr. Braboy started his second year at Little Rock, he was looking forward to continuing his work, even though he had reached his sixty-fifth birthday. One morning, he told Mrs. Stanton he was going to Dillon to take care of some school business. On the corner of Harrison Street and First Avenue, Mr. Braboy was involved in a terrible auto accident. B.P. Gordon, owner of Dillon Wood Works, said that he saw the accident happen and stopped to investigate. In just a matter of minutes, the rescue squad was on the scene, and Mr. Gordon stated that Mr. Braboy seemed to have a serious injury to his head. He was taken to the hospital, and his family was notified of his accident. Mr. Braboy was out of work for several weeks, and his associates said that he never completely recovered from his injuries.

Mr. Braboy finished out the year at Little Rock, but he was not able to continue his work. In 1973, he retired after forty-two years of teaching elementary education in two states. He went home to McColl, but his health declined rapidly, perhaps due to the injuries he suffered in the accident. Ernest Barfield told me he saw Mr. Braboy on the street in McColl about a year before his death, and his mind seemed to have gotten pretty bad. Ernest said that he seemed to remember very little about his days at Leland Grove. James K. Braboy passed away quietly at his modest home on Church Street in McColl on November 14, 1976. He was seventy-three years old. James Braboy spoke often of the "Monster of Ignorance," a creature he fought all his adult life.

His funeral was held at Fairview United Methodist Church, which he had served so well in many capacities. There was a standing-room-only crowd at the small church as many of his former students, fellow workers and friends came to pay their last respects to this extraordinary man. Just a few yards from the church is a small cemetery with about twenty-five graves. This is where James Braboy was laid to rest; he wanted to be buried in the community in which he had served his people so diligently. On December 30, 1992, his faithful wife and friend, Lily Hall Braboy, passed away and was buried next to her husband.

I have visited their graves several times since working on the Braboy story, and one might expect to see a nice memorial at his grave site, but his grave is marked with a modest stone that reads, "HE WAS JUST, HE LOVED KINDNESS, HE SERVED HIS PEOPLE WELL AND WALKED HUMBLY WITH GOD." Next to him, Lily's marker reads, "SHE WAS THE WIND BENEATH HIS WINGS." These inscriptions were chosen by their only child, Dorothy Louise Braboy Madden.

To this day, I still don't know why I chose to write the Braboy story. I guess it must have been something spiritual that caused me to try to bring this man's memory back to life after some thirty years. When I began the story, I knew basically nothing about the man, but now I feel as if I knew him personally. Sometimes in my mind, I can see him walking through the woods from his house to the little country school, or I can see him standing by the chalkboard, teaching his class to write their names. Some very good things came from the Braboy story. When this series of articles was printed, they were put into the hands of a Dr. Pat Maynor, who lives in Lumberton, North Carolina, by none other than the widow of the late English Jones. Dr. Maynor is of Indian descent and has a strong passion for the Lumbee tribe. In just a matter of days, she got in touch with me and said she was moved by the Braboy story and wanted to do something in his memory. She

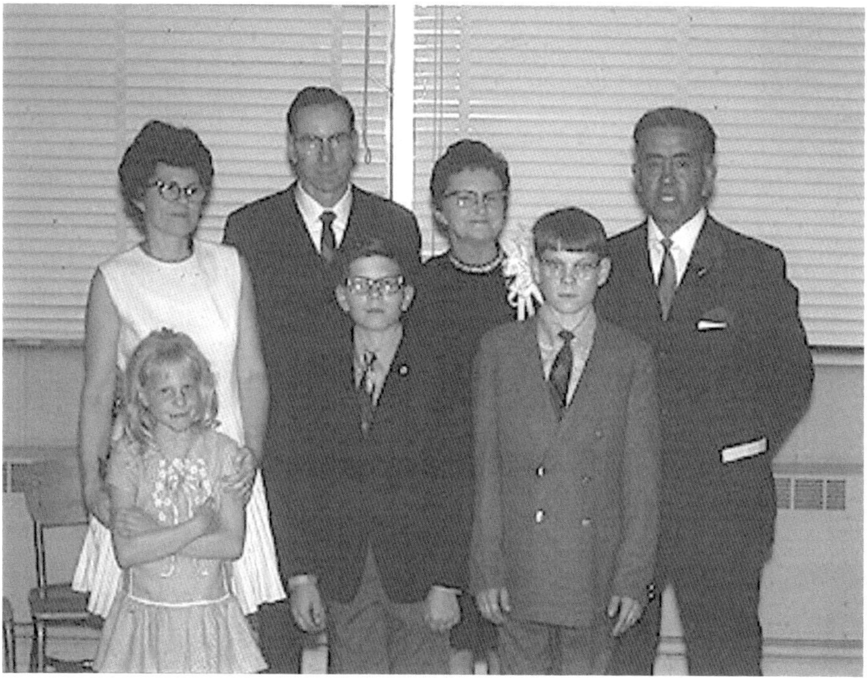

Family of James K. Braboy. *Courtesy of Cecil Madden.*

was an alumna of UNC–Pembroke, so she decided to start an educational scholarship in his name. She and her father, Mr. Cleo Maynor, opened the endowment, and we went to the college for the photo shoot and the presentation of the check.

Since that time, a group of ladies in the Carolina Community who have a quilting club made a beautiful handmade quilt for the endowment, so we sold tickets and had a raffle, and we were able to add some money to the scholarship. It is my sincere hope that I in some way may be able to keep this man's memory alive. We are working to have a memorial marker placed in the vicinity of the old Leland Grove School to remind people in years to come what James K. Braboy did for the Indian people of Dillon County.

DILLON'S FORGOTTEN SHERIFF, CLYDE SESSIONS BETHEA

The purpose of this story is to try and set the record straight about one of Dillon County's early sheriffs. Sometime back, an elderly gentleman, Mr. Alford Campbell, called me and asked if I could help him on a matter. I told him that I would if I could. He told me that there was a sheriff back in the early days of Dillon County that just seems to have been forgotten about.

He said this man's name was Clyde Sessions Bethea, but that he was not listed in the *History of Dillon County* or any of the *Dillon Herald* editions that covered the history of Dillon County. Mr. Campbell, who is now ninety-four, said Bethea was sheriff back in the early twenties, because he had a tax receipt that belonged to his uncle that was signed by Clyde S. Bethea and dated 1921. In that time, the sheriff also collected taxes.

We visited with Mr. Campbell several times and made copies of old documents relating to this sheriff in question and discussed this man that seemed to be forgotten. I looked at our copy of the *History of Dillon County* and sure enough, there was not a Clyde S. Bethea mentioned. It shows our first sheriff, S. Vernon Lane, serving from 1910 to 1924 and then Walker Allen from 1924 to 1942.

The first person I approached was the present sheriff, Harold Grice. He said he knew about Sheriff Bethea and that he and Deputy Allen Berry had done some research on him because he wanted to have a plaque made with all the names of the sheriffs that had served in Dillon County. Sheriff Grice said he didn't know the exact dates that he served and would be thankful for any help that we could give him. Well, I put my chief researcher, my wife Helen, on the job, and after some considerable research, this is the story.

In 1910, when Dillon became a county, there was an election held March 15, 1910, to elect our first office holders. In the first primary, there were seven men who ran for sheriff. A runoff was held on March 24 between Stephen Vernon Lane and J. Dudley Haselden. Lane was elected our first sheriff by a vote of 1,051 to 918. Lane was elected twice after that, and in 1920, he ran for reelection again, but this time there were five men in the race. The first primary was held September 2, 1920, and Lane led the ticket, but a run off was necessary between Lane and Clyde S. Bethea. In the first primary, there was a Don C. Martin who got 350 votes, and in the run off on September 16, 1920, it seems that the most of Martin's votes went to Bethea. Clyde S. Bethea was elected Dillon County's second sheriff.

In 1924, Bethea ran for reelection, and this time it was a four-man race that included Walker Allen. Again, a run off was necessary between Bethea and Allen. In the run off, Bethea was reelected by the narrow margin of 20 votes—1424 to 1404. In July 1927, after some serious health problems for a good while, Clyde S. Bethea had to resign the office of sheriff. I don't know exactly the nature of his illness, but he was in a sanatorium in Columbia, which leads me to believe that he may have had tuberculosis.

Coroner Baker Gasque, who served Dillon County as coroner for fifty years, and was also blind, took over the sheriff's office. The county delegation asked for a special election, but in August 1927, Governor Richards appointed Walker Allen sheriff, a job he would hold until 1942.

To give you a little more history on Sheriff Bethea, he was born October 5, 1882, the son of L.T. Sessions and Mary Elizabeth Smith Sessions. Shortly after his birth, his mother passed away. Mr. and Mr. Joseph James and Caroline Pearce Bethea, who were cousins of the family, cared for the infant because Mr. Sessions had several other children.

In time, the Betheas would adopt the child and give him the Bethea name. Clyde S. Bethea graduated from Wofford College and studied law, but chose to get into politics instead. It was said that he was popular among his followers.

A little less than a year after he resigned as sheriff, he and a friend, Will Allen, were on a fishing trip a few miles from Marion when Mr. Bethea told Mr. Allen to take him to the shore because he did not feel well. As Mr. Allen was rowing to shore, Mr. Bethea stood up and fell out of the boat. Even Mr. Bethea's oldest living relative, Mr. Wade Sessions, thought that the former sheriff drowned, but Mr. Allen was able to keep the sheriff's head out of the water until he could get him to shore.

The coroner ruled the death as natural causes. He was thought to have had a stroke. Clyde Sessions Bethea died at the age of forty-three. He is buried at Magnolia Cemetery at Latta. He was married to Josie Pearl Bennett and had three children: Carolina, Martha and Joseph Bennett. His daughter-in-law, Iris Moody Bethea, lives in Dillon.

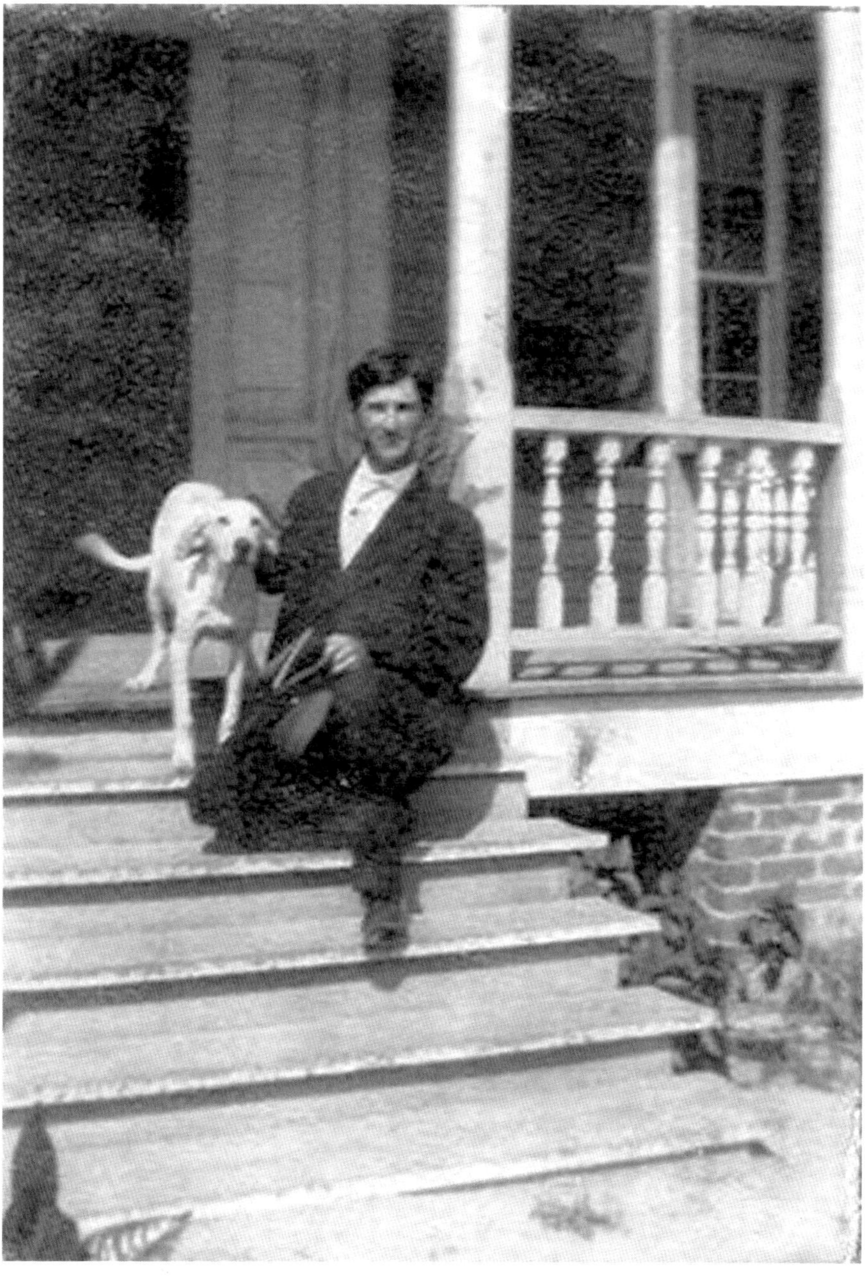

Clyde S. Bethea: the Forgotten Sheriff. *Courtesy of Martha K. Dudley.*

My question is: how could a man who was duly elected twice by the citizens of Dillon County just fall through the cracks and not be remembered anywhere? I think that we need to set the record straight and give this man his rightful place in the history of Dillon County.

For what it is worth, both Sheriff Lane and Sheriff Bethea's obituaries are wrong on their dates of service. I need to thank Mr. Alford Campbell for bringing this matter to my attention. Had it not been for his interest in a man he didn't even know, this matter might have never been brought to light.

LITTLE ROCK, A DILLON COUNTY LANDMARK

Just five miles west of Dillon on Highway 9, you will find the small community of Little Rock, Dillon County, South Carolina. Like a lot of small towns, if you blink while passing through, you might miss it. Little Rock has one caution light where Harllees Bridge Road crosses Highway 9, and at that crossroads is a stone buried several feet in the ground. This is where the town got its name of Little Rock. A lot of people pass through Little Rock during the summer months, going to and from the beaches, but little do they realize the rich history that this small community has.

Little Rock was first known as Harlleesville, named after one of the first settlers in this area. Thomas Harllee, a young man from Virginia, along with his mother and sisters, came to this area with only the clothes on their backs after the Revolutionary War and settled on the banks of the Little Pee Dee River, perhaps near where Harllee's Bridge is now located. Harllee and his family had left Virginia when his father Peter Harllee died and left the family impoverished. That part of Virginia had been so ravaged by the war that Harllee knew the family needed a place to start over.

Thomas Harllee came to this area with only the will to work and to try and make a better life for his family. He had mechanical skills and began a boat- and flat-making business because most of the transportation was done on the river. The business began to flourish, and soon he opened a mercantile store on the bank of the river. Harllee began to buy land along the Little Pee Dee. He sold his flats to rice planters and loaded his pole boats with merchandise for his store on the Little Pee Dee. This was the only store between the Marion Courthouse and Cheraw.

He entered into farming and breeding of stock and bought all the land on both sides of the river for several miles. When Harllee came to South Carolina, he could barely read and write. The family was too poor to buy candles, so he studied by the light from the fireplace. Thomas Harllee became self-educated and served as clerk of court for the Marion District

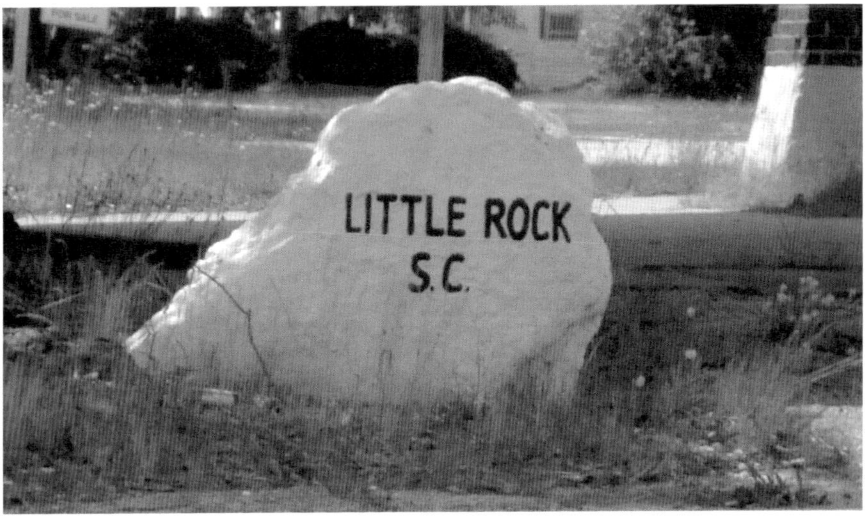

The Little Rock stone at Little Rock, South Carolina. *Photo by Helen Wiggins.*

from 1810 to 1826. He amassed a fortune and married Elizabeth Stuart, and they raised ten children together. Many great military people descended from the Harllee family, including Andrew Harllee, a Civil War hero.

There is a Harllee family cemetery just a few yards from Harllees Bridge, Little Rock, in Dillon County, South Carolina, where many members of this family are buried. In 2004, the Andrew Harllee Camp of the Sons of Confederate Veterans did a tremendous job of cleaning and restoring this historic cemetery. Why and when the name of Harlleesville was changed to Little Rock is unknown, but it may have been when the Harlleesville Post Office and the new Little Rock Post Office combined in 1853.

Just how old is Little Rock? Little Rock is the oldest settlement in what is now Dillon County. On March 8, 1872, Little Rock became the first town in upper Marion County. In 1786, Francis Asbury, a Methodist Circuit Minister, started a church in a brush arbor in Little Rock that became known as Liberty Chapel, later to be called St. Paul's Methodist Church, which served the Little Rock community for many years. The church is a historical building today, having been placed on the National Register of Historic Places in 1977. Unfortunately, the church no longer has services due to the declining population in the area. A large cemetery surrounds the church, with many of Little Rock's oldest citizens buried there.

Little Rock has a rich history indeed. In 1853, the founding father of our county, James W. Dillon, opened a mercantile store in Little Rock, and despite the financial setback by the fall of the Confederacy, accumulated a respectable estate. Later, Dillon would move to the town that would bear his name. There is not much left in Little Rock today that would remind us that this was once a thriving community, but who knows—maybe with the right moves, this Little Rock could have been like the town in Arkansas that bears the same name.

Little Rock had been chartered as a town some forty years before Dillon became a county. When the county of Dillon was born on February 5, 1910, Little Rock put in a bid to become the county seat. Mr. J.W. Hamer—whose family came from Marlboro County and became wealthy landowners and businessmen in the Little Rock area—put up $25,000 to erect a courthouse in Little Rock, but the town of Dillon, which was founded in 1888, was chosen over Little Rock due to its better railroad access.

When the county was founded, Little Rock had a larger population than Dillon: three hundred in Little Rock and two hundred in Dillon. Little Rock has had a post office since 1853, when the Harlleesville Post Office, which was established in 1807, became the Little Rock Post Office. John G. McKinnon became the first postmaster of Little Rock, and James W. Dillon was postmaster from 1859 until 1866. Little Rock still has a post office today; Joyce Braswell Page was appointed postmaster in 1979, a job she still holds today.

Back in 1985, the late Alan Schafer, perhaps the most successful Little Rock citizen—a man who took a roadside drive-in and turned it into one of the best-known tourist attractions on the East Coast, a business that we know today as South of the Border—wrote a very descriptive history in a special edition of the *Dillon Herald*. Mr. Schafer's father, Sam Schafer, was born in Little Rock in 1888.

Mr. Schafer stated in his article that in the 1920s, Little Rock was a thriving little town. There was a train depot with passenger waiting rooms, a storage dock for loading and unloading the train and a telegraph service. Next to the depot was E.P. Mobley's store, followed by Greenspun's Hardware and then the Bank of Little Rock, the old massive white brick building that later housed the offices of Schafer Distributing Company for many years. Next was the two-story Little Rock Hotel, presided over by Mrs. Lula Driggers.

On the ground floor of the hotel was A.D. Pope's store and Mr. Russell Thompson's drugstore. In the next block stood Alan Schafer's grandfather's store, simply called the Schafer Company. There was a store operated by Mr. Benny Iseman, where all the kids bought their penny candy. Across the street was Mr. Rufus Cain's store, who was also the postmaster at that time. Next to B. Iseman's store was the Little Rock jail, a clapboard building about fifteen by twenty feet, with two barred windows.

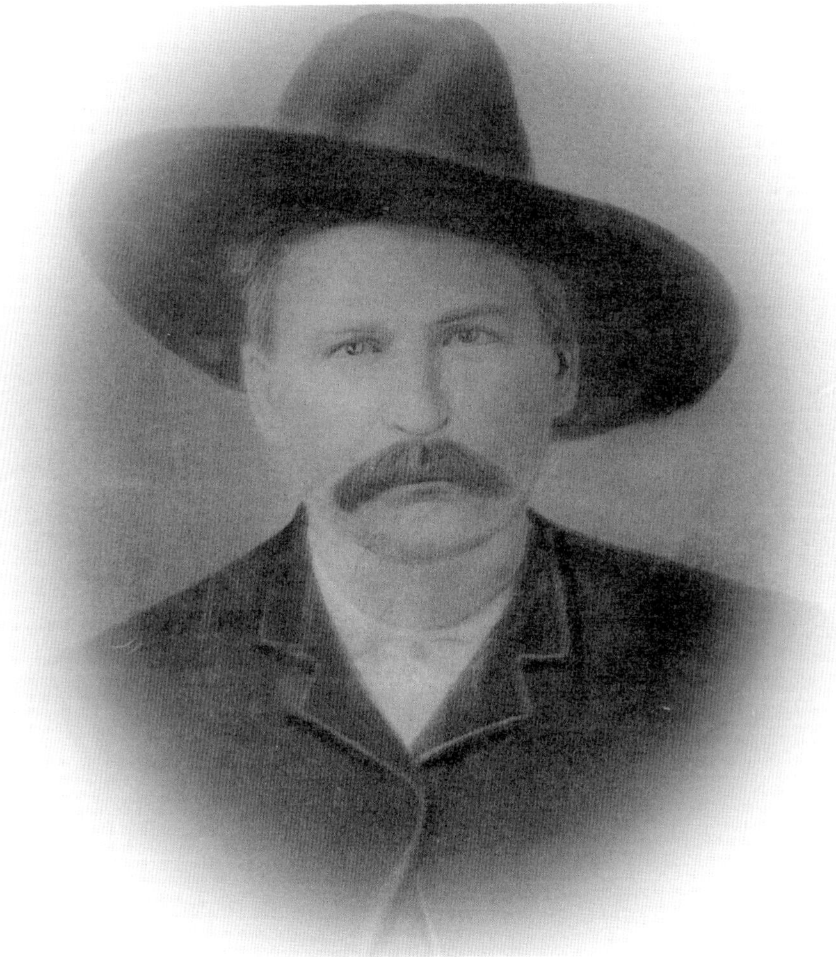

Sam Schafer, 1920s. *Courtesy of Norman Norton.*

Little Rock had two livery stables; Mr. R.H. "Hamp" Wiggins operated one. It was said that Mr. Wiggins would go to Missouri and buy his mules and have them shipped back by train. Mr. Sam Britt owned the other livery stable. Mr. Britt was the father of Mr. Herbert Britt, who became a successful attorney and was in the South Carolina House of Representatives.

There was a dry cleaners, and tailor shop operated by Mr. Jessie Cook, one of the first African American businessmen in the county. Cook had only one leg but was never hampered by the use of it. It was said that he was a leader among the African American community. Then there was Harrison Black's barbershop, which was a meeting place for the local citizens. Bish McColl

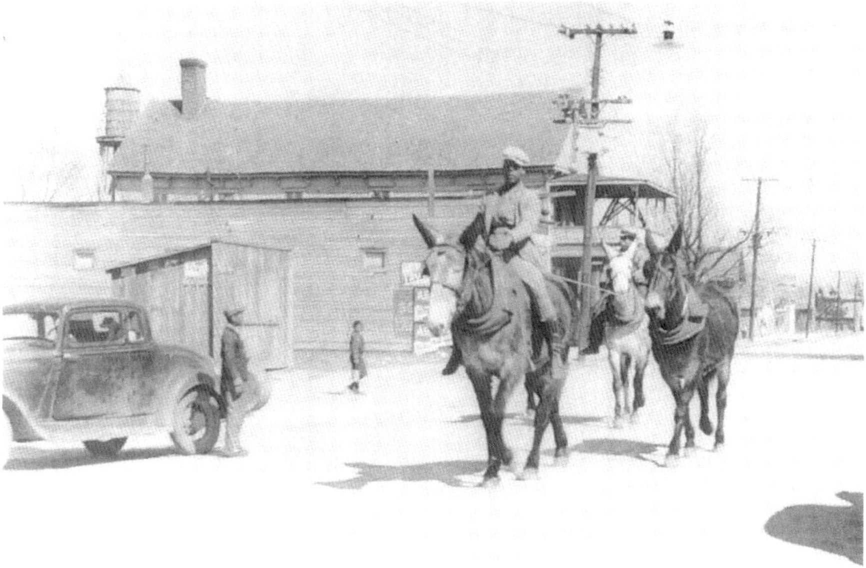

Main Street, Little Rock, 1930s. *Courtesy of Judge James E. Lockemy.*

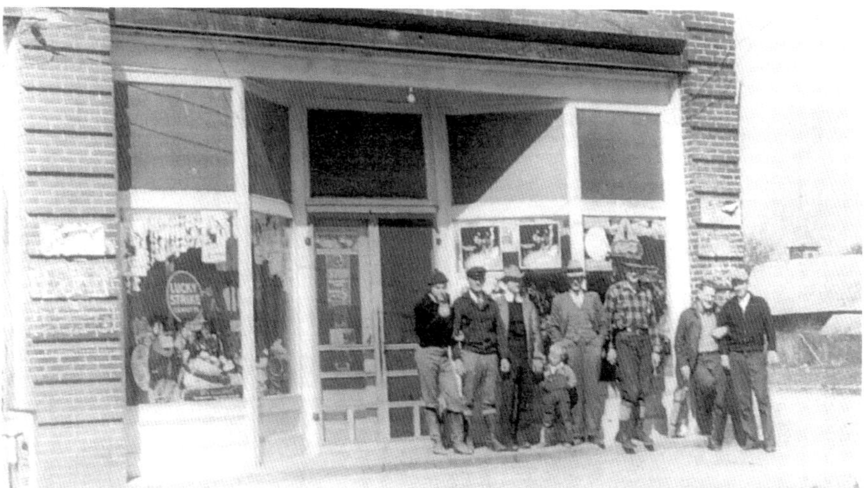

Sam Schafer's Store, 1930s. *Courtesy of Judge James E. Lockemy.*

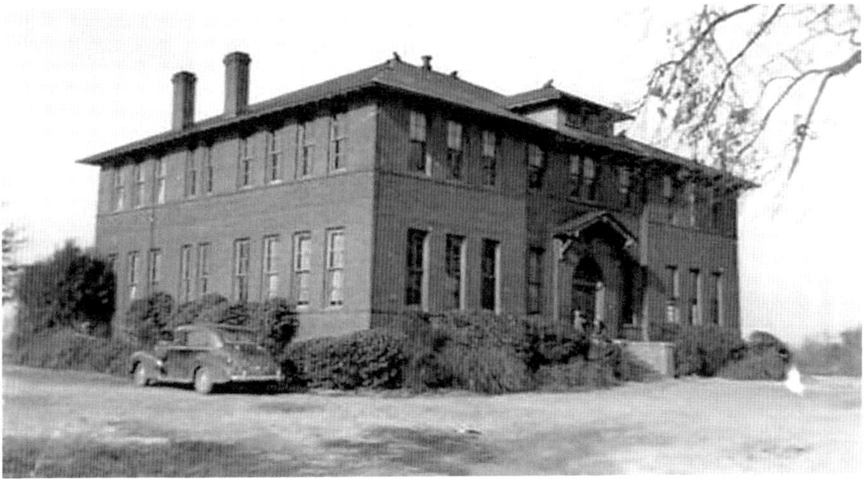

The old Little Rock School. *Courtesy of Hardy Huggins.*

ran another longtime business on Highway 9. The two-story building on the corner of Main Street and Highway 9 was a store run by Alonzo Bethea. Mr. Bethea was of Scotch-Irish decent and was said to have a quick temper.

Little Rock had a cotton gin, school and several churches.

Only two of these churches have stood the test of time, Little Rock Baptist Church, founded in 1885, is still serving the community today. Dr. Richard Alderman has been the pastor for the past forty-eight years. McCoy's Chapel United Methodist Church has an African American congregation and has been a thriving church since its beginning in 1892. Reverend Ronald McCall has been the pastor for eight years.

The once-thriving small town called Little Rock is nothing more than a memory now, but what a rich history it holds; I can envision the bustle of business on the streets of Little Rock, where Alan Schafer opened his first business at the age of eleven years. It was an ice cream stand that he opened on Saturday. The ice cream would come by train from Buttercup Ice Cream Company in Hamlet, North Carolina. He would sell $6.00 in ice cream on Saturday and make $1.25 profit.

Fifty years later, he would open an ice cream parlor at South of the Border, and guess what kind of ice cream he sold? You got it—Buttercup. That ice cream store would gross $10,000 a week in the summer months, a long ways from the little stand in Little Rock. Little Rock is just a small community you ride through on the way to North Myrtle Beach, but it could have become the county seat of Dillon County and perhaps the largest town in the county had things gone the other way.

REEDY CREEK SPRINGS, A ONCE-FAMOUS RESORT

Since I have become involved in researching some history for the past couple of years, it is amazing what I have found out about people and places that I never knew existed. The place I will attempt to write about in this story was once a very popular resort that drew a lot of people, but this was some thirty years before I was born and I had never heard of it.

I was born and raised about five miles from Reedy Creek Springs, but the popularity of the springs died out before my time. Reedy Creek passed about a mile from my home, and I remember as a boy fishing there for "Red Fin Pike." We would put a small piece of "fatback" on a hook with a line and cane pole, then we would tie a piece of red cloth to the hook and "jigger" for these pike. Am I talking above your head? These were tasty little fish that you could fry real crisp and pull the backbone out, and you could eat the rest of the fish.

Reedy Creek Springs is located just a few miles west of Dillon just outside of Bingham off Highway 34 West. There was a historical marker at the point where you turn off to go to the springs, but someone apparently stole the marker. Now just what someone would want with a historical marker is beyond me, but I guess someone thought it would look good in their trophy room.

When I started to research the springs, I had no idea where the resort was located. A fellow named Bob Berry that I was in school with about a hundred years ago called and said he would be glad to show me where the springs were located, because he was reared just a short distance from them. Early one morning, Bob and his brother Jimmy met me at the road to the springs. Bob and Jimmy are sons of the late B.O. and Kate Berry. Mr. Berry was an industrious farmer in the Bingham area, and Mrs. Berry taught school for many years at Dothan and Latta schools. Mrs. Berry taught me in the first and second grade. I never could figure out why she wanted to continue teaching after those two years.

The road leading to the springs was in good shape; Jimmy told me later that his father hauled 150 loads of sand on that road back in the seventies. It was a chilly morning. We had some snow and ice a couple of weeks back, and at one point Jimmy had to stop and cut a small pine tree that was blocking the road. In about another quarter of a mile, we stopped and got out of our vehicles, and just a few yards over in the woods were the once-famous Reedy Creek Springs.

It is nothing more than a small water hole now, but once it was a thriving vacation spot. Back across the dirt road, we saw the steps to the old hotel that was located at the springs and pieces of the concrete walk that led to

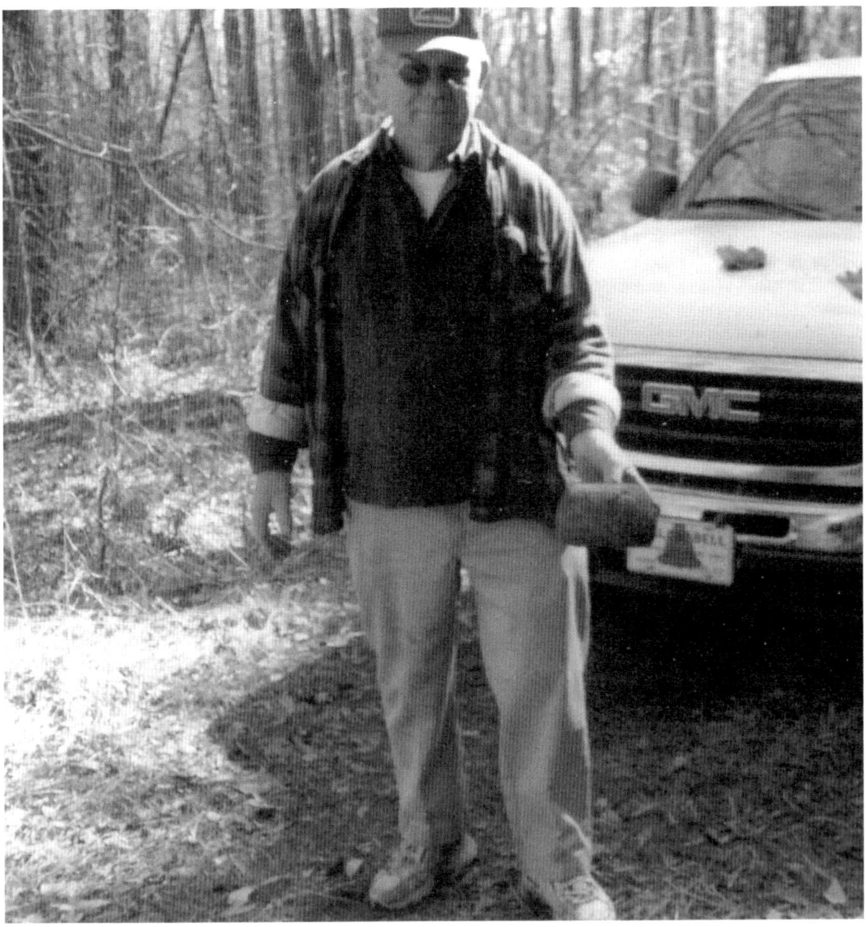

Jimmy Berry holds an old bowling ball found in Reedy Creek Springs. *Photo by Carley Wiggins.*

the springs. These are the only remains of the structures that were located there. Jimmy showed me an old wooden bowling ball that was dug up by a road plow near the springs. At one time, there were two bowling alleys there. The ball was almost flat, from age I guess, and it only had two holes instead of three like today's balls. My guess is that the ball is at least a hundred years old.

Reedy Creek Springs has been traced back as far as the Civil War. As I looked around the location, which is mostly covered with tall pines and brush, I could just imagine what a beautiful spot it must have been back in the time that the springs were so popular. Mr. W.B. Allen purchased 125 acres of land that the springs were located on in 1878. Two rustic cottages and a small structure surrounding the springs, built by former vacationers, were the only buildings on the property when Mr. Allen took the property over. Mr. Allen transformed the springs into a summer resort and "medicinal center."

Twelve cottages were built for rental, and then a twelve-room hotel was erected. The hotel was two and a half stories high with rooms for twelve boarders. The hotel contained a fine dining area, kitchen, servants' quarters, storehouses, stables and porches across the front and back of the hotel. It was like something that you might find at Myrtle Beach today. The springs were about 250 feet in front of the hotel with a concrete walk leading to them. This was a first-class operation for that day and time. There was also a pavilion that was lit by lightwood flares, which also helped to keep away the mosquitoes. All the buildings were undressed lumber except, perhaps, for the floors and casings.

Allen's primary purpose was to develop the springs as a health resort. He had the state chemist analyze the water, and it was found to have a high mineral content. I have heard old people say that the water was supposed to have healing content to it. Another thing that added to its popularity was the railroad that came through Bingham. In 1895, there was a railroad built, extending 19.53 miles from Latta through the communities of Mallory, Bingham, Dunbar and into Clio. The railroad was referred to as the Latta branch. This was before the days of automobiles, and the railroad gave visitors easy access to the springs.

Bob Berry took me on a tour around Bingham and showed me where some of the old sites were located. He said his grandfather, James Franklin Berry, had a cotton gin and lumber mill in Bingham. He showed me where the old post office was located where his father, B.O. Berry, worked at one time. Bob said that his father lived until his mid-nineties and stayed active almost right up to his death. Bob said that every Christmas he would give his

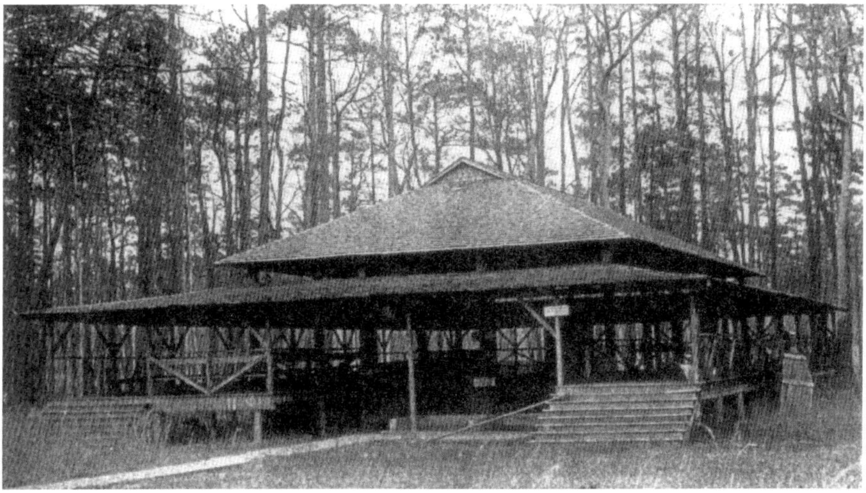

Pavilion at Reedy Creek Springs, late 1800s/early 1900s. *Courtesy of Mamie Cole Gray.*

father a new shovel and by the next Christmas, he would wear it completely out. We saw where the old railroad came through. The tracks are gone but you can see very clearly where the land was built up for the tracks. There was not a depot in Bingham at the time, but there was a water tower where the train would stop to take on water.

Near this location, there was a set of brick steps. In my estimation, this is where passengers would get on and off the train. From there it would have been about a mile and a half to the springs. A buggy would be sent over to pick up the guests that would be staying at the resort. Of course, a lot of people would come by horse and buggy.

Some would come just for a day and some would stay for several days. The springs were very popular for picnics; groups would come from Blenheim, Dunbar, Latta and Dillon. It was reported that people came from four different states to visit the springs. As more and more people came, the responsibilities became greater and greater for the owner. Mr. Allen decided that the springs were taking him away from his other business interests too much.

In 1909, Mr. Allen sold the famous springs and property to Mr. W.T. Bethea and Mr. J.B. Gibson. In addition to operating the resort, these two men organized the Reedy Creek Springs Bottling Works for the purpose of shipping the well-known water for home consumption. The waters of Reedy Creek were known all over for the cure of indigestion, liver and kidney complaints, loss of appetite and many other problems.

In 1910, the partners proudly advertised: "Reedy Creek Springs Hotel, rates $7.00 to $10.00 per week, excellent cuisine, trained servants." The hotel was equipped with waterworks and other modern improvements and screened throughout, with cement walks to and from the springs, wide porches and comfortable chairs.

The springs continued to flourish until automobiles became common, and the popularity of the springs began to decline because people were able to travel greater distances. The Fourth of July was a very popular day at the springs. It was known as "lay by" day. This was when all the crops were laid by, and people would celebrate with a day of rest and fun. Finally, the springs were abandoned and the buildings disappeared. Today, only the buzz of insects and the tinkling of Reedy Creek remain.

I talked to an African American man named Willie Hodge, age eighty-two, who has lived around Bingham for almost all of his life, and he remembered a good deal about the springs. He said he had an older sister that worked there as a young girl. Now, Reedy Creek Springs is just another piece of history gone forever. I can only imagine what it must have been like to get on that train and go to Reedy Creek Springs.

THE DIARY OF JOHN S. MURPHY

What I am going to attempt to write about in this story would have meant absolutely nothing to me two years ago. After becoming involved in trying to trace my family's roots, I have learned that old historical documents are quite priceless. We began to find deeds and documents concerning my family as far back as 1809, and there is no way that I would know as much today as what I do without these old papers. I hope that I will be able to go back much farther, but sometimes it takes years to try to put this history together.

What I want to share with you has little to do with my family. A few weeks ago, Mrs. Mary Mac Carmichael Stephens was kind enough to share a copy of a diary that was kept for a period of about forty years by a man named John S. Murphy. Mrs. Stephens had known about this diary for several years, and she came by it almost by accident because it seems that it was about to be destroyed. She was able to buy the diary for a small sum of money, and to the average person it would have been worthless. To someone interested in the history of Dillon County, South Carolina, it would really be something to cherish.

Mr. Murphy did not go out and buy a diary or ledger to keep his notes in; he used a book that was already printed, called *The Book of Illustrations to Patents Granted During the Year of 1856*. I have seen the book, and it is very tattered and worn. The front and back covers are missing, and many people would have never paid any attention due to its condition, but it contains information that is not documented anywhere else. After obtaining the book, Mrs. Stephens went about the task of trying to learn to read it, because Mr. Murphy wrote across the pages, upside down and in any order that he could fit his notes into the book. These were just little notes he would make about his life and the things that he did in a forty-year period.

I am sure he never thought that anyone would be interested in what he wrote. He did not write in any pattern or order; he just wrote what was in his

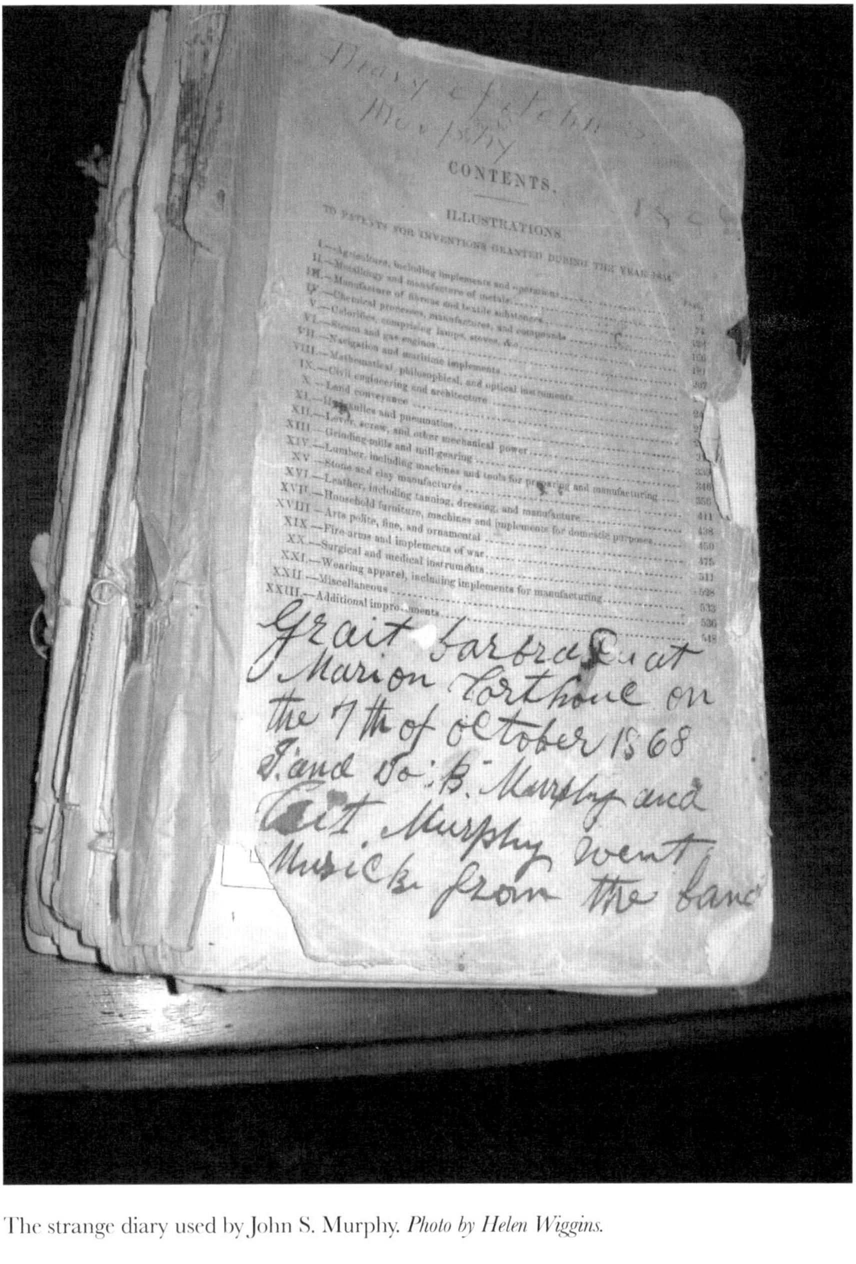

The strange diary used by John S. Murphy. *Photo by Helen Wiggins.*

mind at that particular time. Mr. Murphy had beautiful handwriting. Like many people in that day and time, education was hard to come by, and he wrote the words just like they might sound. For example, he spelled *made* as *maid*, *leather* as *lether*, *great* as *grait*, *pair* as *peir* and so on.

Mrs. Stephens took on the monumental task of copying the book in longhand, which I am sure took years, considering the way that the diary was kept. She did not correct any of his spellings, and that is what makes it so special. There are many things about the diary that I have not been able to figure out, and she will admit that she does not understand it all. But every time I read the diary, I find something new that I can understand.

Mr. Murphy was born in 1824, about eight miles northeast of Dillon just past South of the Border in the edge of North Carolina that is called "the Hall Place." He was a son of Angus Murphy, and at some period of time they moved to the Kentyre section of Dillon County, which was Marion County, South Carolina, at that time. That seems to be where he spent the rest of his life. Mr. Murphy started keeping his diary in 1856, although there are some dates listed as far back as 1842, so he must have transferred these from another book or just had them in his mind.

John Murphy was an industrious man and a jack-of-all-trades. He did many things in his life, and one of the first he mentions is being a shoemaker. It seems that he would go to homes and make shoes, sometimes two or three pair, and often he would spend the night; perhaps it would take more than one day to make the shoes. When he first mentions shoemaking, he was getting two to three dollars per pair. After the Civil War, he was only getting seventy-five cents a pair. He kept records of every pair he made and the amount charged to make them. One year he made twenty-seven pair, and this would vary every year. It seems that getting the material to make the shoes was a difficult thing in that time.

Murphy was also a blacksmith; he mentions making plows and repairing harnesses for mules and horses. He was also a farmer, and he recorded in his diary how many potatoes, corn, fodder, cotton and other items that he would make in a year. He raised livestock and would mention butchering hogs and cattle for food.

Another thing he did was plant a lot of trees and grapevines; he would list the names of the plants and where he would plant them. I haven't counted the number of trees that he planted during the time that he kept the diary, but there were a lot. He also mentions making grape wine and other strong drinks. He made notes about who bought the drink and how much he charged them. At one point, he said he "would sell no more brandy on credit." Undoubtedly some of his customers would buy the brandy and then not pay him.

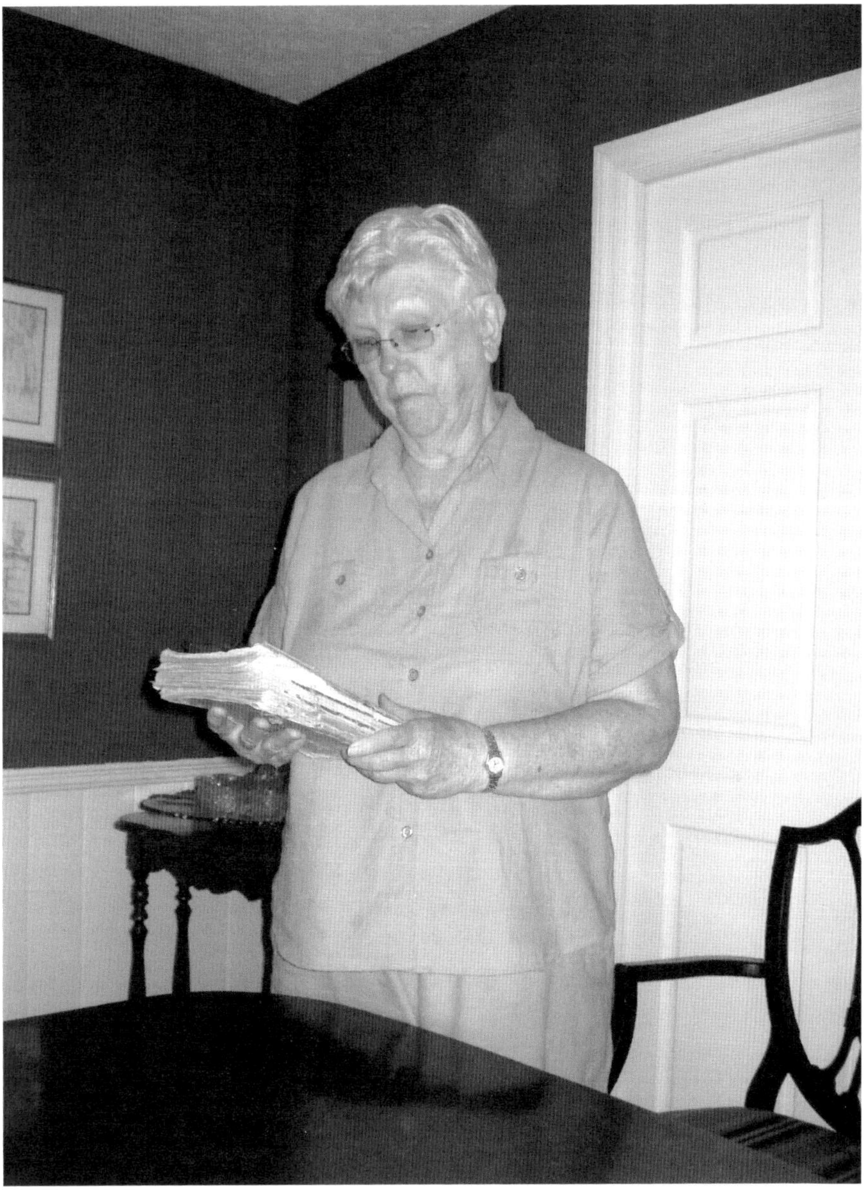

Mrs. Mary Mac Stephens holds the diary of John S. Murphy. Mrs. Stephens recovered the diary and transposed it into long hand. *Photo by Helen Wiggins.*

He also mentions the time that his house caught on fire and burned the kitchen. He said that he rebuilt the kitchen, so he must have also had carpentry skills. Mr. Murphy had much to say about a neighbor named Enos Edwards. It seems that Mr. Edwards took very sick for a period of several months, and Mr. Murphy cared for the man until his death. I was able to come across an old land deed where Mr. Edwards deeded his farm to Mr. Murphy for the love and care that Murphy provided in his last days.

Mr. Murphy mentions no wife or children, but he did have a brother named Joseph B. Murphy, who served in the Civil War and married Caroline Carmichael on March 23, 1871. The brother passed away November 26, 1874. John Murphy recorded all this in the diary. Murphy was always about his work and never mentions being tired, and undoubtedly he was blessed with good health because he does not mention feeling bad or being sick. John Murphy, in my opinion, led a fascinating life.

It seems that he produced everything that he ate from the farm. Mr. Murphy also kept beehives from which he would gather honey. We find several instances where he appraised land and personal property for people, as well as witnessing deeds and documents, so he must have been upstanding in the community. In my opinion, I think the most interesting thing that he did was to take rafts down the Little Pee Dee River to Georgetown.

Now when he first talked about rafts, I pictured something that Huck Finn might have had. But after talking to Mrs. Stephens and reading the entire diary, I found that what he was talking about was actually floating logs down the Pee Dee for different people. What they would do was cut the timber and tie the logs together to form a raft, and then float the logs down to Georgetown. In Georgetown, there must have been a sawmill where they would sell the timber. In talking about these rafts, he would refer to the number of sticks, so the size of the rafts would vary. When you think about it, there weren't trucks in those days to transport the logs, so they had to move them on the river. It would take from about ten days to three weeks to make the trip. Just to quote one trip, he said, "I started on a raft for Daniel Campbell, Duncan Campbell and John E. Campbell on April 8, 1878 and got back on Saturday, April 27th." He was paid fifteen dollars for the trip. He made numerous trips for many different people.

John S. Murphy did so much more by his keeping of the diary than just to tell us what he did for a living. He recorded weather events. On March, 23, 1864, he wrote about a "grait" snow on the ground, it "snode" all day on March 22. He mentioned many names that are still popular in this area today. He talked about Butlers, Campbells, Carmichaels, McCormicks, McDaniels, McIntyres, Millers and many more. He even mentioned two

Wigginses in his writings. He made note of "grait" dances held at various places; he talked about surprise parties and a "grait" barbecue at the Marion Courthouse.

Murphy also kept records of tragic things happening to people, such as his account of the poor fellow that cut down a tree to get a squirrel that he had killed, but a limb fell off the tree and killed the man. He told of a woman that was thrown out of her house for not being able to pay her debts. He told of things that happened during the Civil War, such as deserters being shot or hanged, as well as men who were killed in the war. He made notes of elections being held and the people that were elected. Mr. Murphy must have been a religious man—he had much to say about Kentyre Presbyterian Church. He was very active in getting the church started, and he also notes that in 1871, he donated two and a half acres of land to build the church on. He mentions many church services and even mentions someone being turned out of the church for not living up to its standards.

In the diary, Mr. Murphy mentions many marriages, births and about 250 deaths. In all of these, he would note the dates. This was long before the days of modern communication. Without telephones, radio, television or newspapers in this area, how he gathered all this information is a wonder to me. Sure, most of these people lived within several miles, but I still think that it is remarkable that he was able to record all of this information.

Mrs. Stephens said that she had verified many of these dates from old cemetery markers and so forth, and she had not found anything wrong as yet. John S. Murphy departed this life on March 24, 1896, at the age of seventy-two. I don't think that he ever thought that the things that he recorded in his strange diary would ever mean anything to anyone but him, but I count myself fortunate to have a copy of the notes that he kept over this forty-year period.

I am grateful that Mrs. Stephens saw fit to share the John S. Murphy diary with me. Though the things he made notes of in his strange diary were just for his information, little did he know that he was writing a part of what would become Dillon County history. It would be great and fitting if in the future this man's simple thoughts in their entirety could be published.

DAVID GREENE, A TRUE SURVIVOR

The story that you are about to read is perhaps the most amazing story that has been my privilege to write. From a personal standpoint, I think that the story of David Greene is the most rewarding that I have written.

Over the past twenty years, I have seen David Greene at Herald Office Supply, the place where I have made my living for the past forty-two years. He was always very courteous and mild-mannered, and I could tell he was a man of intelligence. My employer, A.B. Jordan III, always spoke highly of David Greene. I had heard bits and pieces about David, but I really didn't know a lot about him. When I approached him about doing a story about him, he looked at me sort of strangely, and then he said, "Yes, you can write my story." I sat down with David Greene a few days later at his home on Harllees Bridge Road, Hamer, in Dillon County, South Carolina. When we had finished, I felt honored that he would let me tell his story.

David Green was born May 16, 1943, on the Allen Curry Farm in the Alfordsville community in Rowland, Robeson County, North Carolina. A poor African American child, David Greene was raised in poverty on a sharecropper's farm, but managed to graduate from Rowland High School in 1964. In 1965, David went to Charlotte, North Carolina and found employment.

This was during the height of the Vietnam War. In March 1966, David was drafted into the U.S. Army and went to Fort Gordon, Georgia, for basic training.

In November of 1966, David was sent to Vietnam. He showed us pictures that were taken while he was there—many of Vietnamese children—and I could tell that his heart went out to them. He remarked about how poor and underfed they were. David had been in Vietnam for nine months when in August of 1967, something happened that would change David's life forever. His unit was on patrol, checking a road for clearance, and David was the point man, which means he was in front of everybody else.

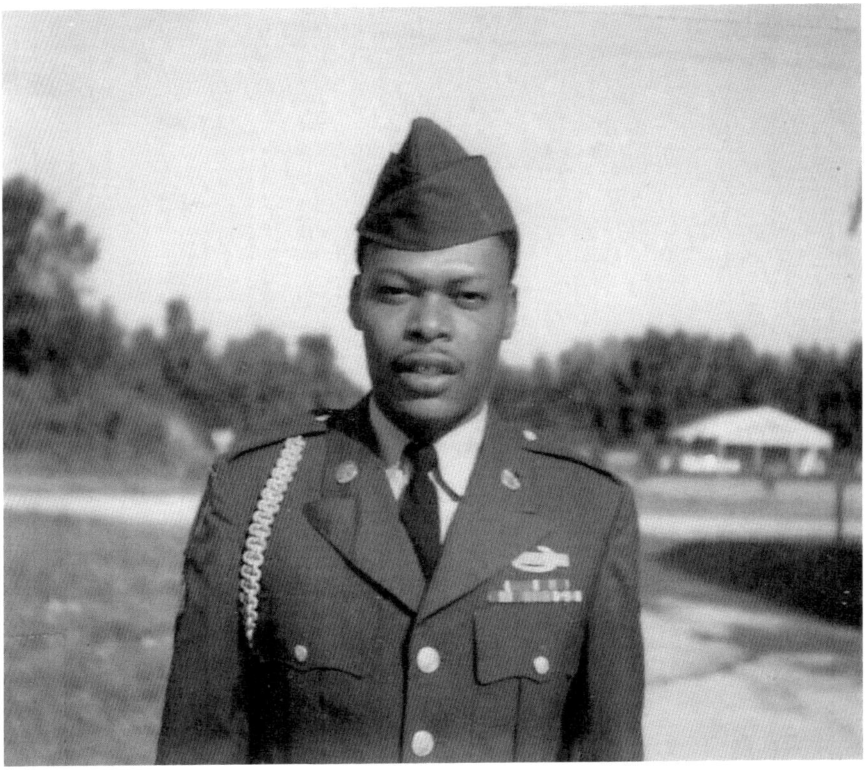

David Greene, the soldier. *Courtesy of David Greene.*

David said he remembered taking the step that put him directly on that land mine. Both of David's legs had to be removed there in Vietnam. From there, he was flown to Germany, and a short time later he was flown to Walter Reid Hospital, where he would remain for nine months. David Greene had two good legs when he went to Vietnam, but he came back with none. David received a Bronze Star, a Purple Heart and a disability that he will take to the grave.

When David left the hospital, he came to the Oakland section of Dillon County, where he has been ever since. David lived with an uncle, John Willie Smith, a tenant on Mr. Tom Kennedy's farm. Like many other Vietnam vets, David had a hard time dealing with life; a lot of people were not kind to Vietnam vets, so he started drinking and tried to forget the war.

Then in 1971, David's life would be changed again. He received Jesus Christ as his personal savior, and has been on the right track ever since. In 1972, he built the house where he now lives, and in 1973, he married Gertrude "Girlie" Dunson. Together they have reared six children. Some folks may know David better by his nickname "Willie B." If you ride out Harllees Bridge Road from Little Rock, you won't have any trouble recognizing David's house. It is the one with the big American flag flying in the front yard.

David Greene has not had legs since he was twenty-four years old. Now I guess a lot of people would feel confined to a wheelchair for the rest of their lives, but not David Greene. David learned to use artificial legs and he learned well. To see him walk today, many people would not realize that he was without legs. He walks with a slight limp, but he has mastered his handicap well, and it is amazing what he has done with his life.

He told us that his first set of legs weighed fourteen pounds each, and he got tired very easily when trying to walk. But over the years, artificial limbs have become much lighter and he is able to move around much better. He told a rather amusing story about a time when he was crossing the street, and when he stepped off the sidewalk, one of his legs broke. He asked a man standing nearby if he could give him a hand, that he had broken his leg. A woman who was standing close by said, "Yes he did, because I heard it pop." She did not realize that it was not a real leg.

I told you that David and his wife had raised six children, but the amazing thing is that five of the six have served in the military. David said that he had never encouraged any of his children to join the military, but I guess that the example he set enticed them to serve their country. A daughter, Regina, is a career U.S. Air Force sergeant serving in Iraq. A son, Gregory, is an Army Specialist Four, serving in Iraq. Another daughter, Watasha, is a reservist at Fort Bliss, Texas. Yet another daughter, Christina, is a teacher in Baltimore and also serves in the reserves. A son, David Jr., works for the United Parcel Service (UPS) in Myrtle Beach and daughter Katrina is a manager for Gap at Myrtle Beach.

Five of the six attended college, and Regina received several degrees while serving in the air force. I asked David how he had such good luck with his children, and he answered, "When we went to church, our children went to church; when we went to the beach, our children went to the beach." To show you what kind of a man David Greene is, after losing his legs in Vietnam, and being home for a few years, David became bored and wanted to go to work. He was receiving disability social security, and when he told his doctors that he wanted to give up the disability and go to work, they were against this and told him that he was making a mistake. David was convinced that he wanted to work. He worked for Fiber Industries in Darlington County, South Carolina; Dillon High School; and the Holiday Inn in Dillon, South Carolina.

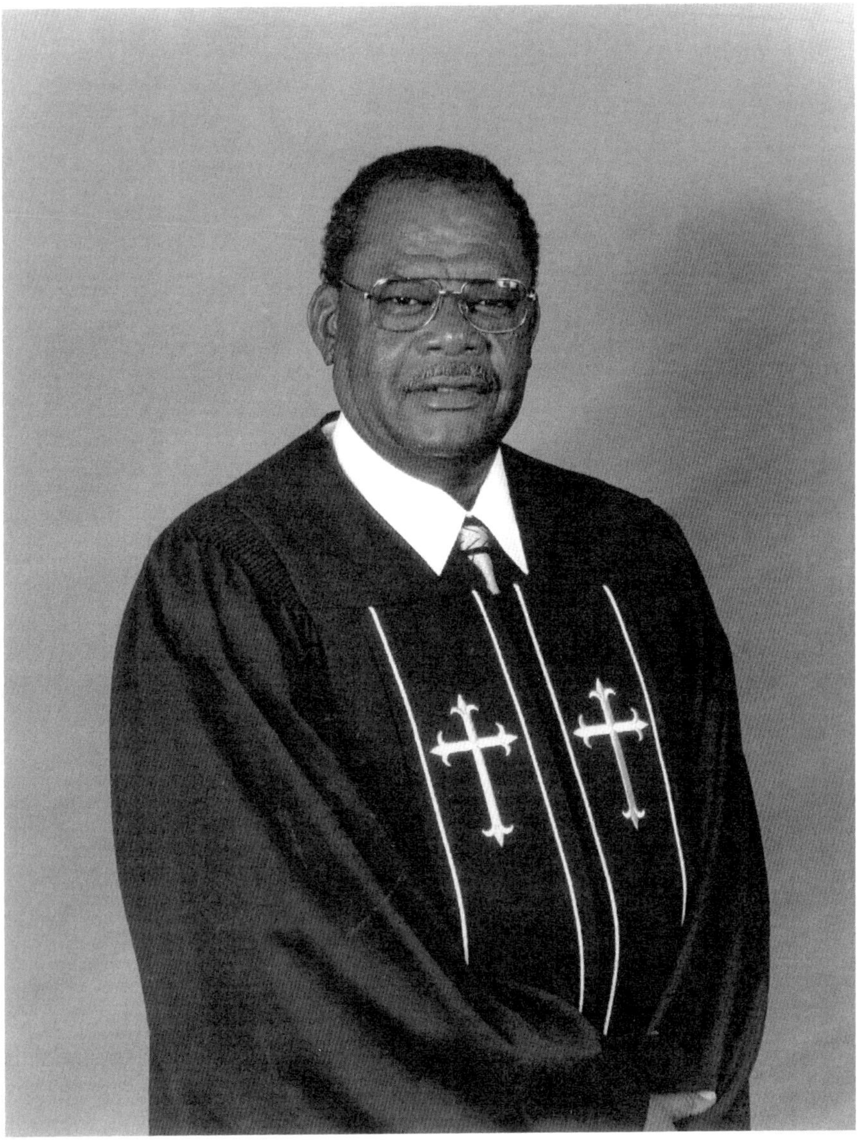

Reverend David Greene. *Courtesy of David Greene.*

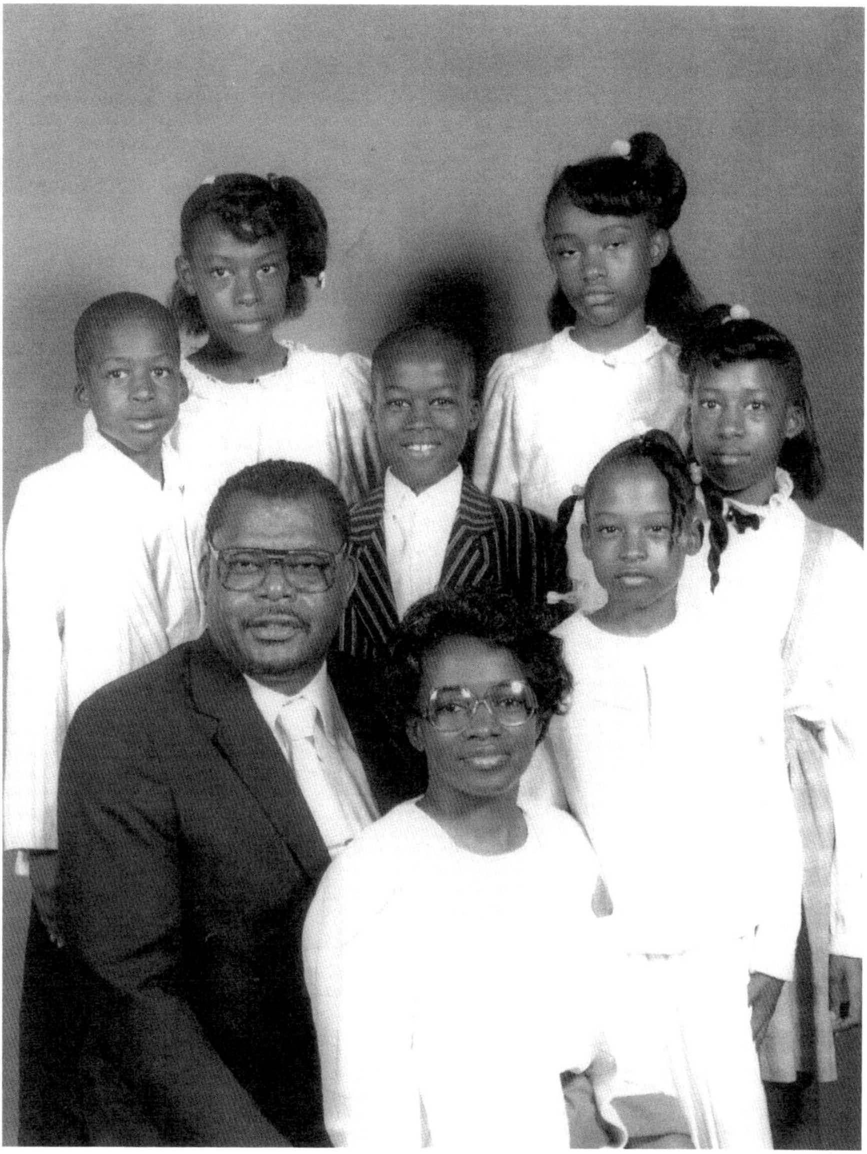

Mr. and Mrs. David Greene and Regina, Gregory, Watasha, Christina, David Jr. and Katrina. *Courtesy of David Greene.*

After about five years, David said that he could no longer stand on his legs for that long period of time, so he had to give up work, and to this day he has never been able to receive disability again. David said that the United States Department of Veterans Affairs (VA) had been good to him and that Veterans Administrator Jerry Huggins at the Dillon VA office has been very helpful. After having to give up work, David thought that he might as well get an education. He attended Robeson Tech, Florence Darlington Tech and Pembroke State University. Today, he holds an associate degree in business.

David is also a licensed minister and an associate pastor. David and his family attend church at Faith Chapel in Rowland. He cuts his own grass, hangs clothes on the line, helps his wife around the house and has been known to ride a bicycle. Not bad for a man without legs. David said that most people had been kind to him over the years, and he mentioned such men as the late Salem Saleeby, the late Tom Kennedy and A.B. Jordan III, CEO of the Herald Group.

David has counseled many young people, and his advice to them, first and foremost, is to get an education. His door is always open to young people who need advice. David Greene's story is the most rewarding story that I have worked on. I am a little older that David, but I myself have learned much from this man, so the next time you feel that life has no meaning, and you feel that you can't go on, think about David Greene, a true survivor.

THE WONDER BOYS

The story you are about to read is about a baseball team, perhaps one of the most unusual baseball teams that I have heard of, but this team may have been one of the best amateur teams to come from this part of the country and just maybe the entire nation.

To tell this story, we will go back sixty-eight years to 1939, the year before I was born. I have heard bits and pieces about this story most of my adult life, and ever since I have been writing articles, I have wanted to research and write something about this team, but I could never come up with enough information to put it together.

Several months ago, I did nine weeks of articles about Border Belt baseball, covering the league from about 1947 until 1963. While writing these articles, I talked to a lot of people, and Kromer Stephens, who played back in the early days of that league, started talking about a country league team from Fork, South Carolina, who went to the National Amateur World Series. I told him that I sure would like to find out something about that team. He told me that he remembered something being published about that team and he thought he had it, if he could just find it. A few days later, he brought me a magazine article about the team that was written in 1992. With the help of that article and some of the relatives of those players, I will try and tell you about the "Wonder Boys."

The class of 1939 at Lake View High School in Dillon County, South Carolina, was special. It didn't know how special as yet, nor how many tests and trials it would face as the world moved toward war. But it was a special class, having won championships both in baseball and football, with most of the teams being from the graduating class. Colleges from all over the state were looking at these boys. However, first came a hardworking summer on the family farms and as much baseball as they could fit in. It was a time when America was thinking about Adolf Hitler and not too much about the future, and America was in love with baseball.

Every little community had a baseball team, and the Lake View boys and some from Fork decided to play for Fork that year under the leadership of Albert Rogers. From the beginning, the Fork team was good, loaded with pure natural talent and a strong desire to win. It didn't much matter that they didn't have uniforms and most of them didn't even have baseball shoes, they simply loved to play the game, and besides, they had as much as most of the local Pee Dee teams of that day. It was only the big city boys that had better, but by the end of the summer the country boys were playing those big city boys.

The farm boys found themselves in the city of Florence in the state eliminations. They marveled to find the baseball field there level, without a cow in sight. Nobody had paid much attention to Fork. After all, they were just a little country league team, and they wouldn't last long. Well, the folks of Florence, South Carolina, found out these boys were for real when they defeated the Florence team easily. Fork was headed to Columbia, South Carolina, where there was a whole city league of teams, and they would be playing the best.

To everyone's amazement, the farm boys rolled over Columbia, and behold, they were in the state championship against Garco, the champ of the Charleston, South Carolina, teams. Garco, it appears, was very big city, too cool to worry about any mismatched yokels from Dillon County. They knew where Dillon County was, having looked it up on the map, but they couldn't find Fork. Was someone pulling their leg? Was Fork a place or something you ate with? Well, the Garco team found out that Fork was a place, and in three innings they were down by ten runs. They couldn't believe the scoreboard. That Fork team had stabbed them in the hand. Garco rallied and bore down, but the country boys were too much for what most people believed was the best team in the state. The farm boys were now the state champions, but that wasn't the end.

What came next was the Southeastern Regional Championship. Fortunately, the meet was held in Mullins, Marion County, South Carolina, and drew a huge crowd as the Fork team had become heroes among all Pee Dee fans. To win, Fork had to win two out of three against Greensboro, North Carolina, considered one of the strongest teams in the country. Each team took one game each and went to the third and final game. The score was 3–3 in the sixth and Greensboro had the bases loaded. Schubert Hayes came to the mound for Fork, and it appeared that young Hayes was the coolest man in the crowd. One, two, three and the inning was gone. Final score: 4–3. This country team was the Southeastern champion. Little did anyone think at the beginning of the season that this little country league team would be going to Battle Creek, Michigan, to play for the national title.

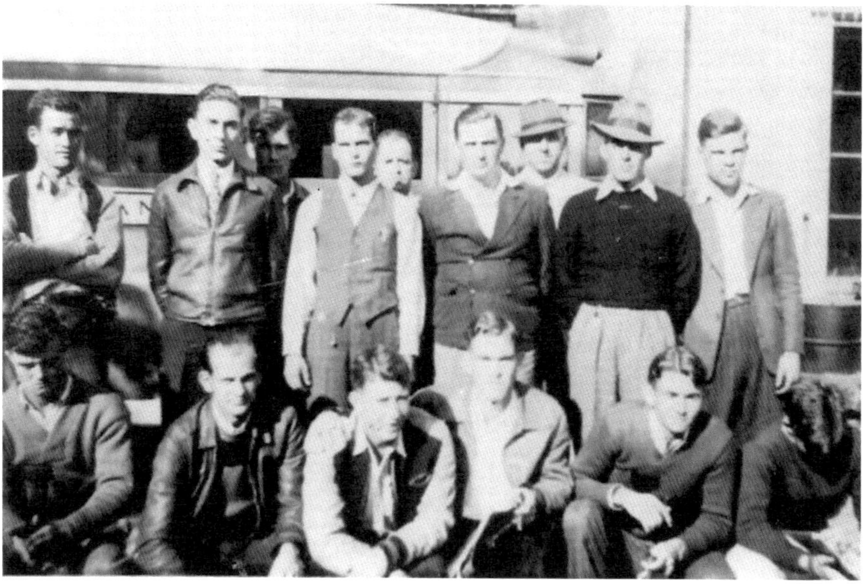

The Wonder Boys: Albert Rogers (manager), Bob Huggins, Maxie Miller, Joe Ammons, Wade Miller, Robert Rogers, Jerry Rogers, Ben F. Rogers, Dick Rogers, Paul Sanderson, Ben Proctor, Hartsell Rogers, Babe King, Bill Moore, David K. Bethea, Pete Rogers, Dewey Proctor and Boyd Carmichael. *Courtesy of Kromer Stephens.*

The team had to be in Battle Creek by the end of that week, but sad to say the team would be two players short. Pete Rogers, the ace catcher, had to report to Clemson for football practice, and so did Dewey Proctor, who would be going to Furman to play football. Proctor went on to play professional football for New York and Chicago and is now in the South Carolina Athletic Hall of Fame. Pete Rogers was sheriff of Dillon County for many years, as well as serving several years as probate judge. This team was so close to winning the national championship, but Rogers's and Proctor's football coaches didn't seem to care too much about a baseball title.

The team left Mullins after being served a country breakfast at Kirby's Drug Store, and arrived two days later in Battle Creek. The Fork boys had never seen such a sight; there was a complex of four playing fields all in one place. The teams all had matching uniforms, and it looked like everybody had baseball shoes. But the dream had gone on long enough. As one player said, "It was like the New York Yankees going into the World Series without Joe DiMaggio and Yogi Berra."

The Fork team went down in defeat against one of their first opponents, but they had nothing to be ashamed of. They had come a long ways in that summer of 1939. Only two of the players are surviving, brothers Jerry and

Dick Rogers, both in their eighties, but their families, friends and old-time baseball fans still talk about the 1939 Fork baseball team that almost won it all.

In respect, these were the "Wonder Boys": Manager Albert Rogers, Bob Huggins, Maxie Miller, Joe Ammons, Wade Miller, Robert Rogers, Jerry Rogers, Ben F. Rogers, Dick Rogers, Paul Sanderson, Ben Proctor, Hartsell Rogers, Babe King, Bill Moore, David K. Bethea, Pete Rogers, Dewey Proctor and Boyd Carmichael.

BOOTLEG WHISKEY

Growing up as a boy back in the forties and fifties in Dillon County, there were many people who made a living making bootleg whiskey. Some called it white lighting, some called it moonshine and others called it stump hole liquor. It was illegal, of course, just as selling drugs is today.

There were small-time bootleggers as well as big-time bootleggers. From what I could see and what I was told by some people that were bootleggers, it was very hard work, and they were always afraid of being caught by the law enforcement.

Bootleg whiskey was made in what was called a still, and they were several versions as I could gather. It usually consisted of a vat in which the ingredients were placed to "work." The mixture consisted of grain bran, sugar, yeast, lye and water. The concoction had to "work" for several days before it was ready to distill into raw liquor. The vat had burners which were lit when the mixture was ready, and the mash was brought to a boil. The liquid then ran through a copper pipe called a condensing coil that goes through a cooling trough. Steam condenses in the pipes and trickles out as high-proof whiskey into half-gallon fruit jars. The drink was usually cut with water before it reached the consumer.

I have heard of other methods such as running the liquid through a car radiator, which usually had lead in it and was said to cause health problems.

It has been said that a professional bootlegger took a lot of pride in what he did and would not sell any whiskey that he would not drink himself.

I had occasion as a teenage boy to run across a still while hunting with a cousin. Lucky for us, there was no one around. The vat was full of mash, which was "working." After taking a look at that vat and seeing the things that had fallen in or crawled in, I knew in my mind I would never drink bootleg liquor. I knew several people back then who were bootleggers, of whom I will not mention any names, although most are dead. I heard stories of how they would carry these fifty-pound bags of sugar and heavy bags of grain into the

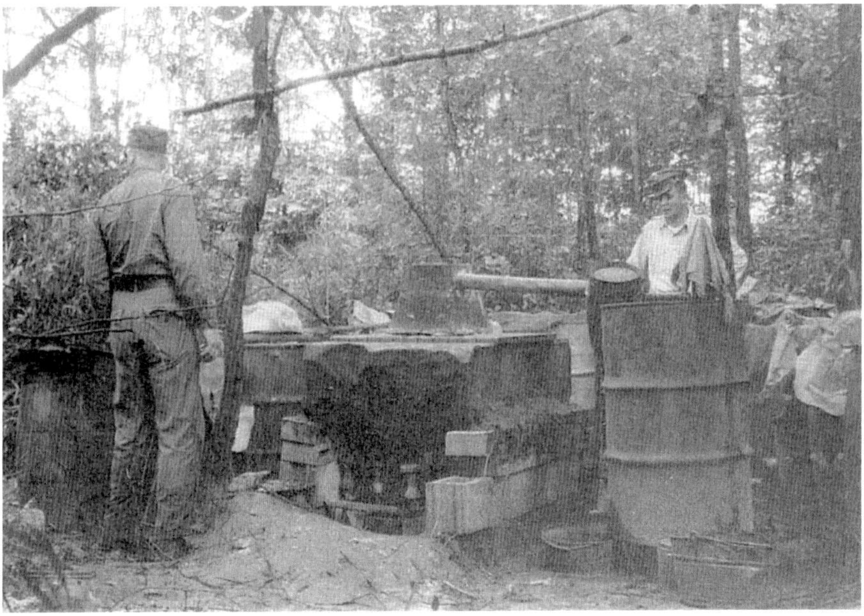

Agents raid a whiskey still in Dillon County. *Courtesy of Lucille Easterling.*

deep woods, mostly at night, because it was safer at night. One fellow said in my presence that whoever thought making liquor was easy was crazy.

After the whiskey was made, it was put in half-gallon mason jars. It would be delivered to customers or kept in a hidden place near their home for sale. A half-gallon of bootleg whiskey back then sold for about three dollars. I never knew a big-time bootlegger, but I was told about men who would haul truckloads to people for resale.

There was also big business for the people who sold the ingredients that went into the making of illegal whiskey. I worked at a country store one summer, and I remember there was a side room where the sugar and other items were kept. There was a door that led to the outside, and I remember loading the bags of sugar and grain into the pickup trucks and the trunks of their cars.

When the sheriff's office and the state law enforcement division began to clamp down on bootlegging, they also began to clamp down on the merchants. If you sold a person a fifty-pound bag of sugar, you had to record their name. I doubt seriously that you could find a fifty-pound bag of sugar in Dillon County today. Sometime in the late fifties, Sheriff Pete Rogers and his deputies began to come down hard on the bootleggers. They would find a still and confiscate the copper and fuel tanks, and then dynamite the

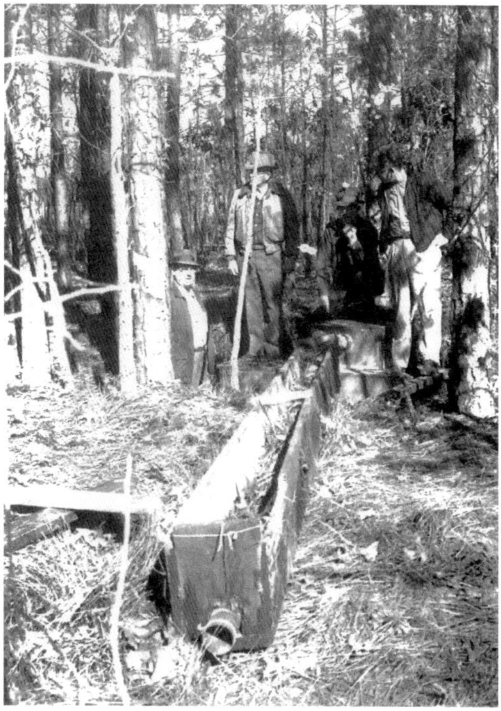

Another still goes down in Dillon County. *Courtesy of Lucille Easterling.*

rest. In 1957, there were seventy-four stills destroyed in Dillon County, and 678 gallons of illegal whiskey and 29,900 gallons of mash were destroyed. There were also many arrests made, with fines and forfeitures amounting to $22,269 just for that year. That was a lot of money in 1957.

Bootlegging still continued to prosper until about the mid-sixties, when the sheriff's department and the South Carolina Law Enforcement Division (SLED) made a huge raid on the bootleggers of Dillon County. I remember going past the National Guard Armory one day, back when the armory was where the City County Complex is located today, and there were a large number of men in front of the armory. I asked someone later what was going on. They said there had been a large liquor bust, and all these men were apprehended. It was said that a young SLED agent had gotten to be friends with one of the largest bootleggers in the county and actually moved into his home and helped with the liquor business. He worked undercover for about six months and collected all the information he needed to put a lot of people away. When the time was right, he called in all the other agents and arrested the bootlegger, most of his family and a lot of his associates and customers. A good portion of these men got jail time, and that bust almost broke the back of bootlegging in Dillon County.

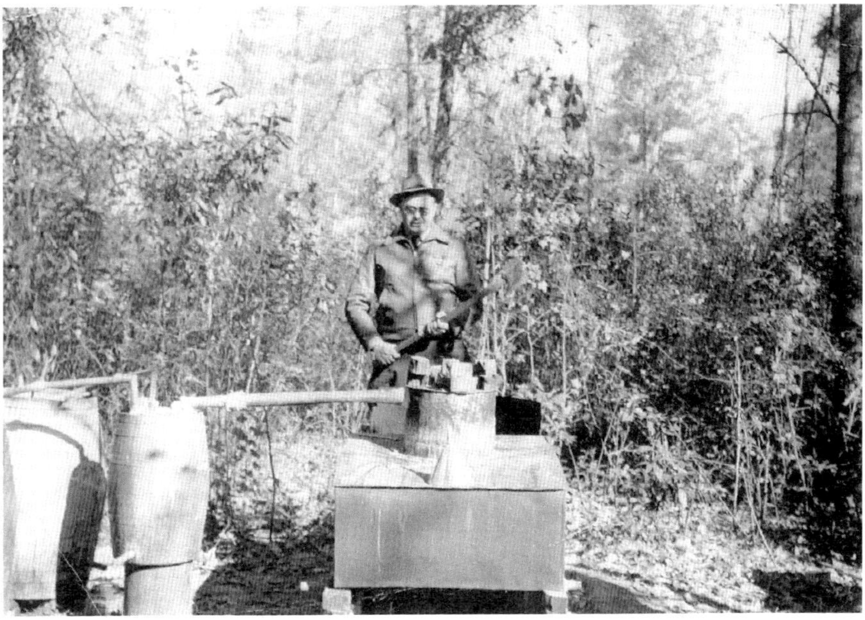

Yet another still is destroyed in Dillon County. *Courtesy of Lucille Easterling.*

Bootlegging continued for a while, and the bootleggers found more secret places to hide the stills, such as in a barn or a hole that would be dug into the ground and then covered with chicken wire. When they left the still, they would cover the wire with leaves and brush. Some people would just have a small still hidden near their home just to make the whiskey that they would drink.

To my knowledge, bootleg whiskey is a thing of the past in Dillon County, and I say good riddance. Former Sheriff Pete Rogers and his deputies, Major Moody and Harley Allen, are pictured in one of the photos, Deputy Jim Thompson is photographed alone and all are deceased. One of the men who worked very hard to rid this area of bootleg liquor is retired Deputy Sheriff Arthur Quick. Arthur is probably the only man still living who helped to drive the bootleggers out of business. Arthur is in his mid-eighties and has been retired for quite a while. He can really share some stories about busting moonshine stills in Dillon County. He said that he enjoyed every still that he helped to destroy, because he knew that a lot of this whiskey had elements in it that were destroying lives. Arthur is convinced that people in this county died from drinking this bootleg whiskey. Now if we could only get rid of the drug dealers, but this is a long uphill battle.

REMEMBERING THE DILLON REDSKINS

A few days ago, an old friend of mine, Jimmy Meekins, came into the store and walked back to my desk and said, "Carley, I have a story for you." He handed me a copy of an old football program from 1962 about a semipro football team that Dillon had back in 1962 and 1963. When I saw the program, I remembered the team, which I had not thought about in years. Jimmy and I talked for a while, and when he left I laid the program over to the side. Later on that day, I picked it up and began to read about some of the players that were on that team, and I made up my mind right then that this was a story I had to do.

I am approached by many people wanting me to write different things, but I have to feel right about something before I will write the story. This is one story that I am glad I chose to write, because it is a story that relates to Dillon history, and also a story that has been good for me personally. I have had a medical problem for several months now and have been down in the dumps. As I began to talk to different men who played on the team and some of the managers and coaches, everybody had a funny story to tell about the Dillon Redskins, some of them really hilarious, which I will share with you as the story unfolds. My wife, who knows absolutely nothing about football, said she was glad I decided to write this because she hadn't heard me laugh so much in months.

This is the story of the Dillon Redskins. In 1962, a group of Dillon men decided to form a semipro football team and become affiliated with the Eastern Carolina Football League. Lloyd Meekins and Harold Gene Jackson were the managers or owners of the team. The coaches were Herbert "Monk" Meekins, line coach, and Eddie Strickland, backfield coach. The team started in October of 1962, and they would play on Saturday nights and sometimes Sunday afternoons when the weather got too cold. Lloyd said that they had players coming from all over the area wanting to play football.

Some of the players had played college ball, some had played high school ball, and Lloyd said he thought some had never played on a football team before. Some were good players and some were just fair players, but they all just wanted to play football. A lot of players might just play one or two games and decide this was too rough for them, because in this type of game, things could get pretty rough, and maybe the rules were not enforced too strictly.

I will try and mention as many of the Dillon Redskin players as I know about and some of the stories that have been told to me. Other teams that were in the league were the Charleston Rebels, the North Charleston Sports, the Mount Pleasant Eagles, the Summerton Indians, the Sumter Generals and there were teams from Orangeburg and Gaffney that the Redskins played against.

The Redskins lost their first two games and decided to enlist the help of a young coach, Bob Rankin, who was probably just starting his coaching career at Dillon High School at that time. Keep in mind, folks, that we are talking forty-four years ago. I called Coach Rankin, who now is retired from coaching and lives in Columbia. I don't remember having a more enjoyable conversation with anybody in a long time. I never met Bob Rankin, even though I followed his career for many years.

We talked as though we had known each other for years. When I asked him about the Dillon Redskins, he laughed and said that this was a real bunch of characters, and even though he didn't coach the Redskins very long, he remembered the names of the players, and had some funny stories to add about a lot of them.

Coach Rankin said they went to Charleston one night to play the Charleston Rebels, and of course they had no bus, so everybody carpooled to make the trips to the games. He said that when they got there, they realized that they didn't have a quarterback, so they had to make out with what they had. He remembered that some of these men were older than he was. There were some of these players in their mid- to late thirties and some as young as their early twenties.

Rankin said that at halftime, the smokers would go off to one area, and the nonsmokers to another area. He said this was not something he was used to in high school coaching. He asked about a lot of the players, and I filled him in as best I could. Of course, some of the players are deceased. But he remembered every one of them. Coach Rankin was real high on a player he thought was from the Clio area named Doug Carlton. He believed that he was a pharmacist. But he had fond memories of his time with the Redskins; he said it was a little different than anything he has ever experienced.

Bob Rankin coached high school football for forty-five years, and he said if he had not had a family to support, he would have coached for nothing—that is how much he loved the game. Bob Rankin earned many awards during his career and is a member of the South Carolina Athletic Coaches Hall of Fame. Coach Rankin is now seventy-four years of age and has one of the most phenomenal memories I have ever experienced. He is one class act.

Under Coach Rankin's leadership, the Redskins began to improve on offense and defense. The Redskins dropped their first two games, but by game three the Redskins were ready to play and walloped the Mount Pleasant Eagles by a score of 45–0. John Cotter scored on a seven-yard touchdown from Gerald Hasty, who played at East Carolina. Cotter rushed for two more touchdowns and the Redskins had a 21–0 lead at halftime. Johnny Rogers raced for forty-five yards in the second half for another Dillon score. Jerry Church recovered a fumble in the Mount Pleasant backfield and went in for a score. Charles Prince scored on a twenty-five-yard pass, and Buck Jolley and Paul Moody nailed the visitor's Bob Evans in the end zone for a safety.

Mount Pleasant's deepest penetration of the night was to the Dillon 49 as the Redskin's defense really shined. Leading the Redskins on defense was Jerry Church, Paul Moody, Norm "Kinky" Hyatt and Buck Jolley, who played college ball at Wake Forest. At the Redskin's first home game, there were about one thousand people in attendance, so the Dillon folks were very interested in having a semipro team in Dillon.

The Redskins had a pretty good year for their first season in 1962. The team went through a lot of players during the first year. Some would come out and join the team, but after a short while they would decide that this was just not for them. A lot of the players only played high school football, but there were several that had played some college ball. Some of the teams that the Redskins played against had some pretty big guys and a lot more that had played college ball.

The Charleston Rebels, for instance, had some heavy hitters, such as Jerry Nettles, who played quarterback at the Citadel and was all Southern Conference; also they had a tackle named Harry Rakowski, who was also all Southern Conference and was known to be one "bad dude." Harold Caulder played both years for the Redskins, and Harold was one of the few people I know who was raised as poor as I was. Harold might not have had a lot of natural talent, but had as much heart as anybody you will find. The Redskins were playing the Rebels one night and the coaches put him in to block Rakowski. Rakowski weighed 260, and Harold weighed 160. Harold said every time that Rakowski hit him, it was like being hit by a truck. Harold said that one time when Rakowski hit him, it turned his helmet completely around on his head, but Harold held his own with the big man and the Redskins came out on top.

I'll tell you about the guys that played for the Redskins, and I hope you will recognize some of the men. I will have to admit that I didn't know a lot of the players, but I will tell you what I have been able to find out. The quarterbacks on the team were Gerald Hasty, who was from North Carolina and played college ball at East Carolina. Someone said they thought he became a coach. Cecil Snipes played some football at Newberry, but I know very little about him. Richard "Monkey" Christmas played quarterback at Dillon High School and would ultimately become the Redskins' main quarterback. "Monkey" was a hard-nosed little guy who was as tough as they come. "Monkey" has been living in Omaha, Nebraska, for most of his adult life. J.B. Carter played some for the Redskins and came out of Dillon High School. J.B. lives in the Laurinburg, North Carolina, area.

John Cotter was a guy who came from up north and played college ball at the University of Toledo, Ohio. Cotter must have been a good running back because in one game, he scored three touchdowns. When he was in the Dillon area, I understand he sold insurance. A standout player for the Redskins was Johnny Rogers, who is a local guy and played high school ball for Dillon. Johnny played both years for the Redskins and was one of their best players in 1963. Johnny is still working today at the McLeod Medical Center in Dillon, where he has been for a long time.

John Williams, a man that I have known for a very long time, played high school ball at Dillon and played with the Redskins until he joined the service in 1963. John played defensive back for the Redskins. He is retired from the paper mill in Florence and lives on Hardy Circle in Dillon. John is a dedicated Christian and is very active in his church and is also engaged in mission work.

Richard Harper was from Marion, where he played high school ball, but I know very little about him. He was a running back for the Redskins. Perhaps the fastest man on the Redskin's team was Paul Prince from Loris High School. I heard about Paul Prince when he played high school football. He only weighed about 125 pounds, but if he got a step on you, he was gone. Paul Prince is on the Horry County Council at this time. Sonny Barwick was a big running back for the Redskins, weighing about 220. Barwick was said to have played at the naval academy, and during his time here was an insurance adjuster.

L.B. Ammons played fullback for the team and came from Marion High School. Several of the people I talked to said Ammons was a good football

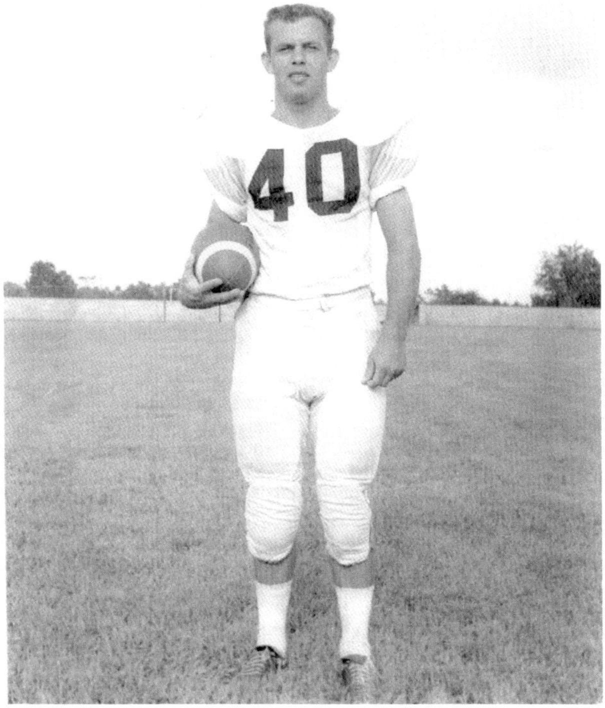

John H. Williams played defensive back for the Dillon Redskins 1962–63. *Courtesy of John H. Williams.*

player. Red Lanier was a highway patrolman in Dillon and played offense and defensive back for the team. Red went to school at the University of South Carolina. The story was told that after a game in Charleston, Red drove home in his uniform with several other men riding with him. Red got pulled over by a highway patrolman for speeding. It was said that Red got out of the car with his football uniform on and went back to talk with the man. When Red came back to the car, he told the others that all he had to do was tell him who he was. I guess maybe he knew the other patrolman.

Paul Moody played one year for the Redskins. He played high school ball at Lake View and also played offense and defense. Paul went on to play with the Sumter Generals and also for a team in Orangeburg before joining the service. Paul now lives between Dillon and Latta and is working on his thirty-fourth year with the U.S. post office. Jackie Carmichael played with Dillon High School and was the punter for the Redskins. Jackie was very active with the rescue squad and fire department in Dillon. He was the son of the late mayor, Billy Carmichael, and is also deceased.

Robert Miller, Jerry Church and J.B. Miller also came to the Redskins from Lake View High School. All these guys were good players, but then Lake View High School has turned out many good football players. Jerry Church

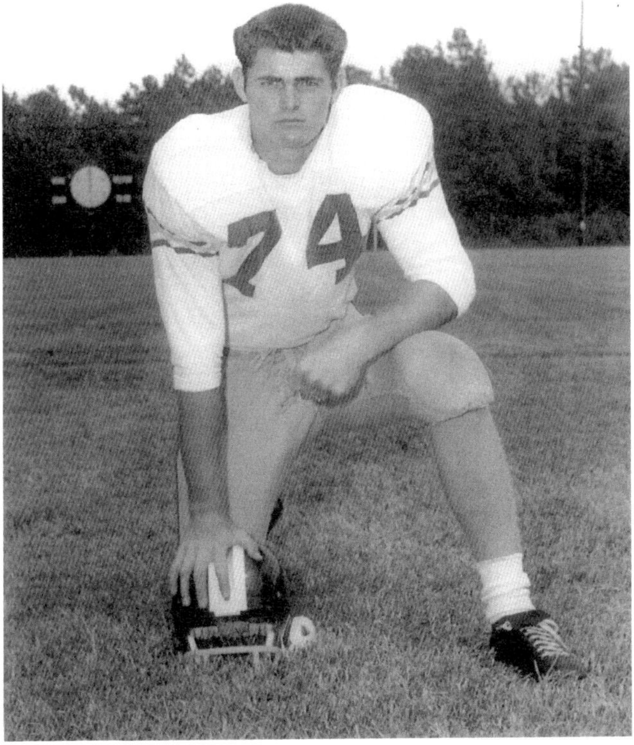

Paul Moody played football for Lake View High School and also the Dillon Redskins. *Courtesy of Paul Moody.*

went on to play with other semipro teams. J.B. Miller owns and operates J.B.'s Jewelry in Dillon. Tom Rowland played for Dillon High School and the Dillon Redskins. Tom is now retired from Wellman Industries and served on the Dillon County Council. He is also active in the "Neighbors Helping Neighbors" organization.

Harold Caulder, whom I mentioned earlier, said that one night, he played seven different positions for the Redskins. Harold is retired from CSX Railroad and lives just outside of Dillon. Harold teaches Sunday school at his church and is also involved in "Neighbors Helping Neighbors." Two outstanding players for the Redskins were Buck Jolley and Frank Thompson. Both of them came from Whiteville, North Carolina, played for Wake Forest, weighed about 230 and played tackle. Gerald Turner, another local fellow who went to Dillon High, played tackle for the Redskins. Gerald was in the automobile business for many years.

Bob Bailey came from Bishopville. Bob weighed over 220, and was said to be quite a ball player. Larry Cannecy came from Marion High School and played center for the Redskins, a job that Harold Caulder would later take over. While talking with Herbert "Monk" Meekins, one of the coaches for the team, he was able to remember some of the players that none of the other men had been able to recall.

There was Teddy Caulder, brother of Harold Caulder, who played linebacker for the Redskins. Teddy retired from the South Carolina Highway Patrol. There was a Jerry Jenrette from Whiteville and Mike Patterson from Cheraw. "Dirk" Rogers from Mullins played with the team. "Dirk" was the brother of "Shot" Rogers, who played quarterback for the Sumter Generals. Bob Perritt played guard for the Redskins. Johnny Barfield, who was a standout player for Latta High School for four years, played for the Redskins for a while. Johnny preferred to stay with the baseball semipro teams because of the danger of injury that football could bring.

David Aston, who was a rough-and-tumble guy, played with the Redskins for a while, but soon found out this was not high school football. Remember, none of these players was insured, though several players were injured during this time. Gerald Hasty, who I mentioned played quarterback for the Redskins, was kicked in the face early in the first year, and that ended his career with the Redskins. Teddy Caulder was taken to the hospital from an

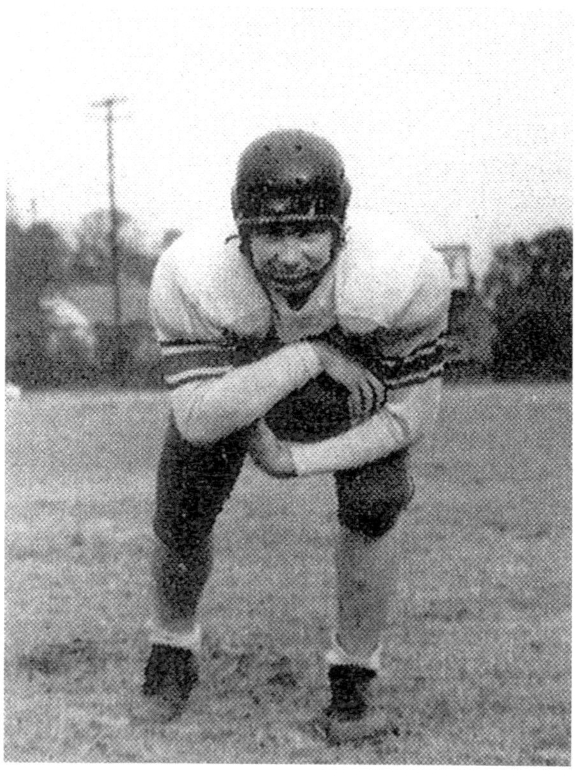

Johnny Barfield played three sports at Latta High School and played football for the Dillon Redskins. *Courtesy of the author.*

injury and was out for a while. Bob Bailey suffered an injury on the field that caused him to go into convulsions. The man was swallowing his tongue, and just as luck would have it, one of the opposing players was a pre-med student who stepped in and perhaps saved Bob's life. There was one instance that a member of an opposing team lost an eye playing against the Redskins. This was not high school or college ball, and some of these players were out to hurt anybody they could.

I would now like to call your attention to perhaps the most colorful character that ever played with the Redskins. His name was Norman "Kinky" Hyatt. I don't really know how much football Kinky had played in his life, but according to his birthdate, he would have been in his mid-thirties when the Redskins were formed. Kinky was a big man, weighing in at 280 pounds. At the first Redskins game, manager Lloyd Meekins, who also served as the announcer, was introducing all the players and where they had played ball as they came on the field. As Kinky came on the field, Lloyd said, "And now from Penn State, oh excuse me, from the State Pen, 'Kinky' Hyatt." There were many stories told about Kinky, and he seemed to be a fellow who loved to have a good time.

One of the officials was a guy called "Shag" Fenters. Shag threw a flag one night, and while Shag wasn't looking, Kinky picked up the flag and hid it under his jersey. Well, after the game was held up for several minutes while Shag looked for his flag, Kinky finally gave it back to him and the game went on. On one occasion, the Redskins were giving away a pony at the game that night, so Kinky rode the pony around town that day to advertise the game, if you can imagine a 280-pound man riding a pony. It was said by game time that the poor animal was sway-backed. Norman Evans "Kinky" Hyatt resided at the Pine Nursing Home for many years and loved for folks to visit him. Don't forget Kinky.

The 1963 season started off with a bang for the Redskins as they blanked Mount Pleasant 26–0. Johnny Rogers scored two touchdowns, and L.B. Ammons gained 173 yards and had one touchdown. Charles Gaddy had come home from the service and added a big punch to the Redskin's game playing at the end position and kicking extra points. Kim Carter had also joined the Redskins at the other end position. "Monkey" Christmas had taken over at the quarterback position and was proven a good leader for the Redskins.

In the third game of the season, the Redskins beat the very tough Charleston Rebels by a score of 19–12. Johnny Rogers ran for eighty yards to give the Redskins the early lead. "Monkey" Christmas passed to Paul Prince for another eighty-yard score. Charles Gaddy kicked the extra

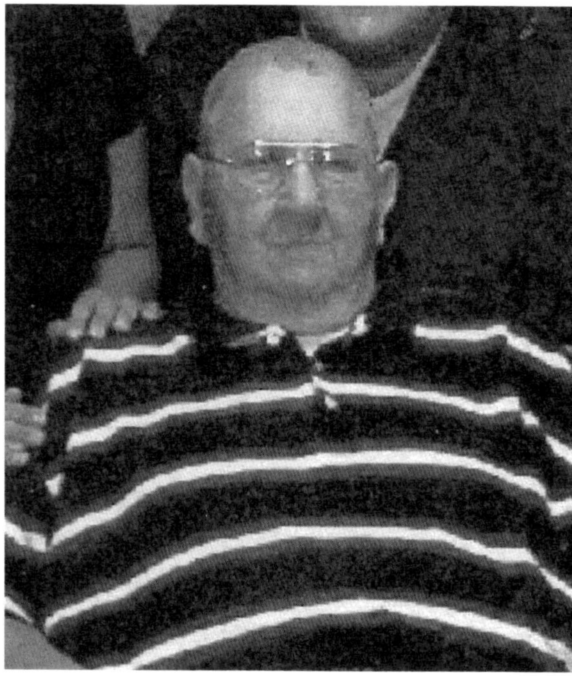

Norman "Kinky" Hyatt was a colorful player for the Dillon Redskins. *Photo by Helen Wiggins.*

points. Gaddy, J.B. Miller and Jerry Church led the defensive effort. In the sixth game, the Redskins faced the Rebels again and came out with a 24–19 victory. Quarterback Christmas threw two touchdown passes to Johnny Rogers for twenty yards and sixty yards. In the fourth period, Christmas blocked a punt, and Charlie Patterson picked up the ball and ran it in for a sixty-one-yard score.

In the final game of the season, the Redskins clinched the league championship by coming from behind to beat the Sumter Generals by a score of 13–10. A seventy-five-yard kickoff return by Robert Miller and the riflelike accuracy of "Monkey" Christmas brought the Redskins from behind to overcome "Shot" Rogers and the Generals. J.B. Miller intercepted a pass to aid the defense, and Johnny Rogers constantly broke through the General line to keep the Redskins in the ball game. Most of the teams that the Dillon Redskins played outweighed them as much as twenty pounds per man, but the Redskins played with a lot of heart and determination.

I don't know exactly why the Dillon Redskins folded—maybe Dillon just couldn't support a semipro team—but for two years the Redskins gave the Dillon fans something to cheer about. It has been a real pleasure talking to some of these old-time football players, and I hope you have maybe learned a little something about Dillon's former semipro football team. Like I said in

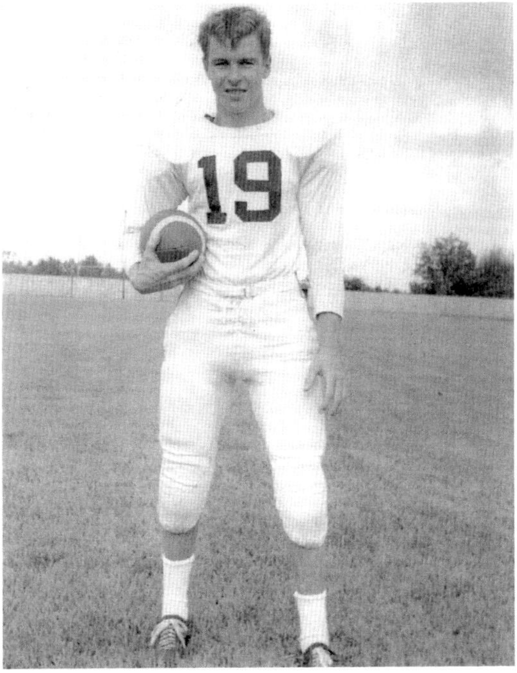

Johnny Rogers was a star running back for the Dillon Redskins 1962–63. *Courtesy of Johnny Rogers.*

the beginning, I don't know the story on a lot of these players, but I would like to mention those who are deceased.

Richard Harper, who came out of Marion, played some good ball for the Redskins. He went to Clemson and became a chemical salesman, and he died at the young age of forty-nine from a heart condition. Lester Webster, who played some with the Redskins and spent most of his life as a mechanic, passed away on September 24, 2003. John Mac "Jackie" Carmichael, the Redskin's punter, passed away on February 2, 2002, and Johnny Barfield, who excelled in three sports at Latta High School and spent many years at Craftex Creations, died on January 16, 2006. Gerald Arthur Turner passed away on December 12, 2006. Coach Edwin "Eddie" Strickland died on January 9, 1994. Since I wrote this article back in 2006, the ever-popular Norman "Kinky" Hyatt died on November 25, 2006, and the Redskins also lost another coach, Herbert "Monk" Meekins, on October 28, 2007.

Dillon may never have another semipro football team, but those old enough to remember will have lasting memories of the Dillon Redskins.

REVEREND MINGO MCRAE, A LIFE OF DEDICATION

The story you are about to read came about by a typewriter, an old Remington manual, that I have been seeing for the past thirty years. This old machine belongs to an elderly black Baptist minister that I only knew as Reverend McRae.

For the past several years, I have had to make Reverend McRae a ribbon for the machine, because ribbons have been discontinued for the machine for many years. I told him several times that he needed to let me sell him a new electric typewriter, but he would say that he was too old to learn to type on a new machine. The last couple of times that he brought the machine in, I would have to get it out of the car for him, because the old gentleman was getting fairly feeble. Just a few weeks back, a younger man brought the machine in, and my first answer was that I didn't have any ribbons for the typewriter, but then I asked, "Is this Reverend McRae's typewriter?" The young man said that he was not able to bring it anymore.

I told the man to leave the machine and that I would make the reverend a ribbon as I had done in the past. Later that day, as I was winding a ribbon for the typewriter, I said to myself, "Old machine, if you could only talk, what stories you could tell."

That is when I decided that I was going to seek out Reverend McRae and see if I could do a story on him. I got in touch with Reverend McRae's youngest son, Lee McRae, and told him what I had in mind. Lee said that his father had been in the Marion Nursing Center since last August, but he had to take him to the doctor in Florence on Monday, and he would bring him by my office. They arrived at 4:30 p.m., and Reverend McRae, who has to use a walker now, came in and sat down. As I began to ask questions about this elderly servant of God, I realized that I was talking to a very special person.

This is the story of Reverend Mingo G. McRae.

Mingo McRae was born October 22, 1913, on the McEachern Farm in the Bunker Hill Community of Dillon County, one of four children born to

Mingo and Sarah Elizabeth McCollum McRae. Mr. McRae was raised poor on a sharecropper's farm and managed to obtain a sixth-grade education at the Saint Luke's Colored School near the North Carolina line.

Reverend McRae said all he ever knew was hard work on the tenant farm where he was brought up. He said he always felt close to the Lord, because his father was also a minister. He felt the call to preach the gospel early in life and began to preach in his teenage years. His first church was Shiloh Baptist Church in Purvis, North Carolina, and his next was Martin's Chapel in Horry County. From there, he went to Old Field Baptist Church in Mullins, where he remained for twenty years. McRae later pastored Effingham Baptist Church in Mullins and Mount Vernon in Horry County. He also served as moderator of the Little Pee Dee Baptist Association for nineteen years.

He stopped being a full-time pastor in the year 2000, having preached the gospel for seventy-five years. After this, Reverend McRae would still preach on special occasions. As I talked to this ninety-one-year-old servant of God, I thought, "What a life this man has lived."

Reverend McRae was married in 1938 to Sarah Thomas and they raised ten children. His sons are Mingo McRae Jr., a past minister of Dillon; Mack McRae of Charlotte, pastor of Oak Grove Missionary Baptist in Pineville, North Carolina; Alexander McRae, associate pastor of the Faithful Few Church of Hamer; Daniel McRae of Oakland, California; Willie McRae of Dillon; and his youngest son, Lee McRae, is church secretary at Hazy Grove Baptist Church at Hamer. Lee made this story possible, with the help of Mrs. Mary Alford Swaner, who put us in touch with Lee.

Reverend McRae's daughters are Ann Campbell of Freeport, New York; Maxie McRae, associate minister of University Park Baptist in Charlotte, North Carolina; and two deceased daughters, Evelyn Robinson and Sarah Jones. He also has two stepsons, Robert Neal of Mullins, and Jimmy Neal of Conway. Reverend McRae's first wife passed away in 1993, and then he married Edith Neal, who still lives in the home. Reverend McRae has more than twenty grandchildren and twelve great-grandchildren. Mingo McRae has preached close to ten thousand sermons in his life and he said he had no idea how many people he had baptized, but that it was quite a few. He told me that he was going to come home from the nursing home and that he was going to preach again. That may or may not be true. Sometime in the not-too-distant future, Mingo McRae will stand in the presence of God, and I don't know if God hugs people or not, but if he does, I believe Mingo McRae will get a big hug, and God will say, "Well done my good and faithful servant. Enter into my glory."

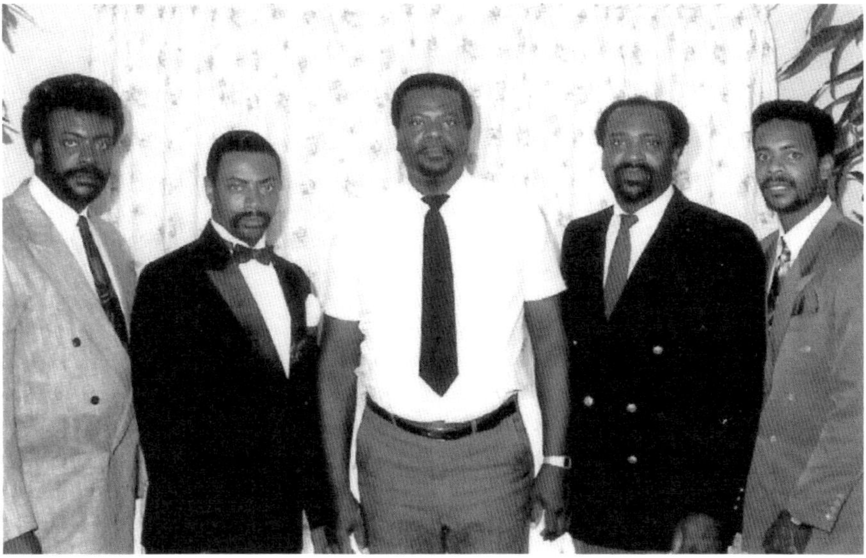

Reverend Mingo McRae's sons. *Left to right*: Daniel, Alexander, Willie, Mack and Lee McRae. *Courtesy of Lee McRae.*

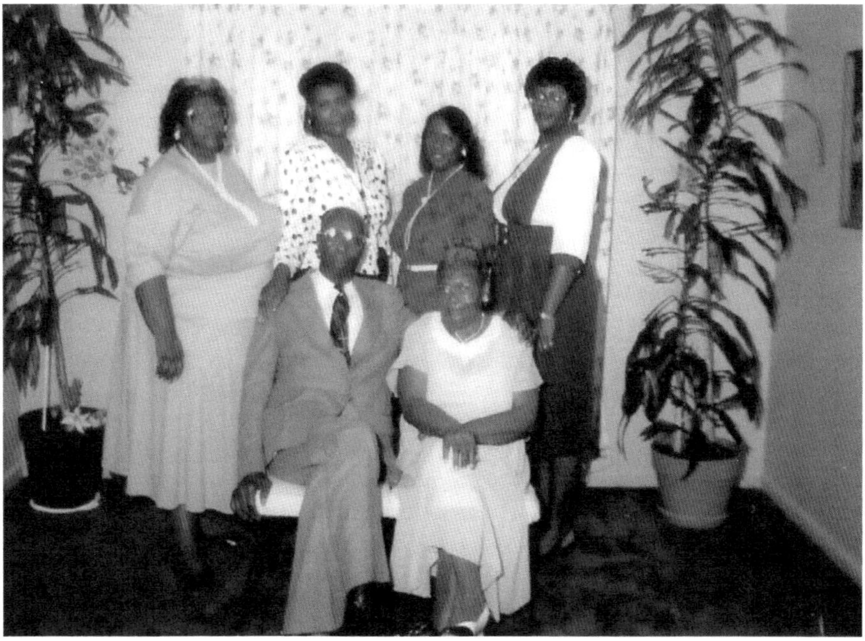

Reverend Mingo and Sarah Elizabeth McCollum McRae and daughters. *Courtesy of Lee McRae.*

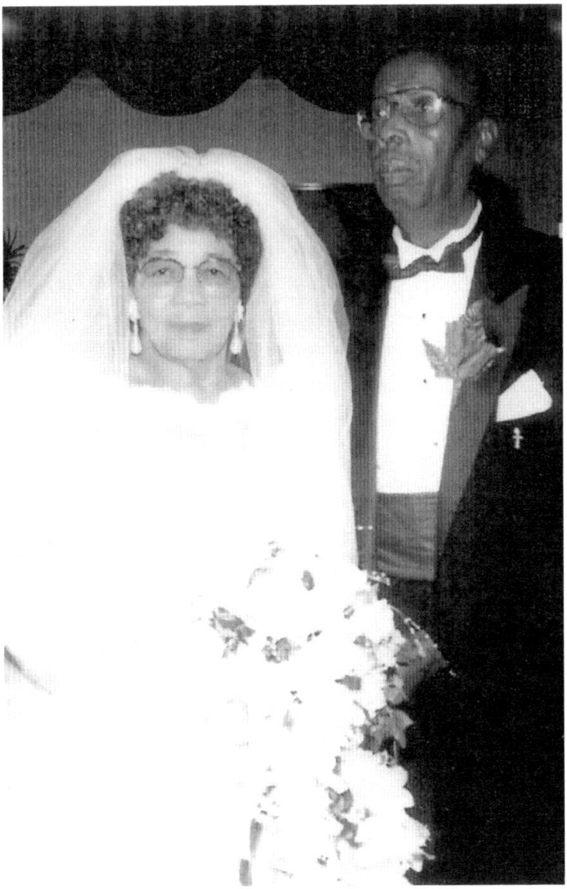

Reverend Mingo and Edith Neal McRae. *Courtesy of Lee McRae.*

As I helped Reverend McRae out to their car, and we put the old Remington typewriter in the back, Reverend McRae asked me, "Sir, do you know what the two saddest words in the English language are?" I asked what they were, and he said "too late," and he closed the door.

As I walked back inside, and sat at my desk, those two words burned in my mind. Think about it, friends.

The Mingo McRae Story: A Continuation of His Life

What you have just read is an article that I wrote some two years before the death of Reverend Mingo McRae. When the article came out, it was very well received by people of all races. A prominent man in Dillon still says it is the best article I have ever written. When the article was published, someone took Reverend McRae a copy of the paper.

The morning after he received the paper, he called me from the nursing home and said, "I just want you to know how much I appreciate this." He told me that he had never had anything written about him in the over ninety years that he had been on this earth.

My wife and I visited Reverend McRae a couple of times in the nursing home, and he was just a joy to talk to. He had these catchy little sayings and riddles that would really make you think. One day, while we were there to see him, he asked, "How old were you when you were born." I had to think for a minute before I said, "I was nine months old." He said, "You are right; a lot of people don't get that one."

On Saturday, January 20, we got a phone call saying that Reverend McRae had passed away. It was two years since I had written the article about him. Most times when I get such news I am saddened, but the only sadness I felt was that I would not see him again. You see, I know what Mingo McRae stood for and I knew what he had accomplished in his life, and I know he is with his Savior.

Some may disagree, but I believe that when Mingo McRae's aged body took its last breath and that old heart beat for the last time, in a flash he stood in the presence of Almighty God, and he didn't go empty-handed—he took a lifetime of service to lay at the Master's feet.

I attended Reverend McRae's funeral at Saint Matthew A.M.E. Church in Hamer, which is one of the largest African American churches in the area, and there was a standing-room-only crowd. Many speakers told of the dedicated service that Reverend McRae had given in his life and how he had touched their lives. The Hazy Grove choir sang songs of jubilation and victory. Reverend McRae had a very large family connection that filled half of the large sanctuary. There was also a large contingent of ministers that had been close to Reverend McRae who came to pay their last respects to this grand old gentleman. I saw some tears from his children and grandchildren, but mostly it was a joyous celebration of a very special life.

Reverend McRae saw so much in his life, having lived through two world wars, the Korean conflict, the Vietnam War and the conflicts we now have in the Middle East. He leaves behind a great legacy for his family and friends to cherish. He touched so many lives during his life. Reverend McRae was ninety-three at his death. Reverend McRae's favorite song was "I'll Go On Living," which simply means that he would go on living in heaven after his death. Reverend McRae was also an accomplished singer with a steady bass voice. The picture that accompanies this story was taken when Reverend

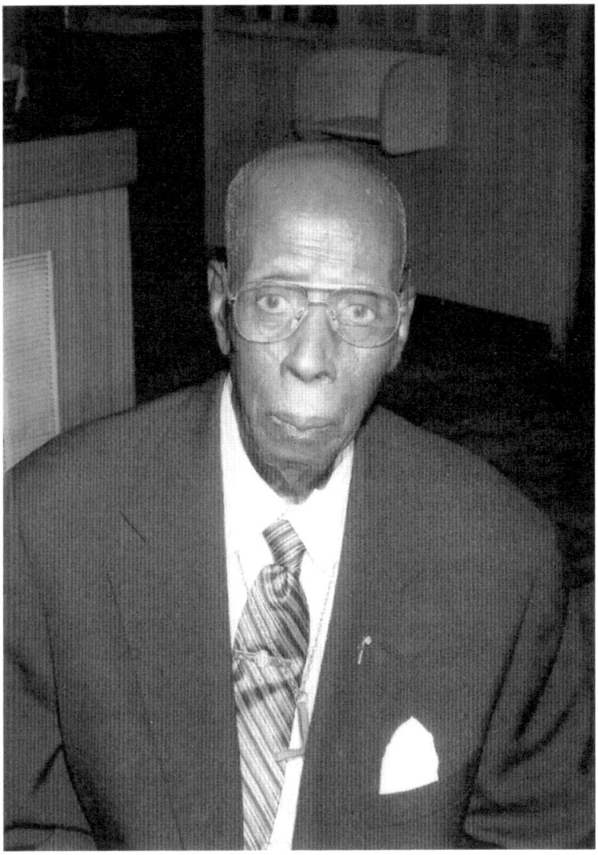

Reverend Mingo G. McRae Sr., age ninety-one. *Courtesy of Lee McRae.*

McRae preached his last sermon on Father's Day 2005 at the Hazy Grove Baptist Church. He was ninety-one at the time. He had to have help to get to the pulpit, and he was only able to speak for about fifteen minutes, but it was a fantastic message.

It was this writer's distinct privilege to hear that sermon. I would just like to add that I count it an honor to have known such a man. The world would be a better place to live in if there were more Mingo G. McRaes.

THE LAST TAXI DRIVER

Since I began writing newspaper articles a few years ago, it has been my intention to write articles about people and places that everybody else has not written about. I like to write about people who have done some pretty great things in their lives but have never had much recognition for the things they have done. We have folks right here in our county that have great stories about their lives that have never been told.

This story is about such a man. When I first heard about this man, the idea just jumped out at me, and I knew that I wanted to write about him. Robert McRae was born on the Fourth of July 1925, about three miles west of Dillon, near where Dillon Furniture Manufacturing Company is now located. He was born a poor African American youngster to parents Dewey C. and Leasie McBride McRae.

The McRaes were tenant farmers and raised six children; Robert was the third oldest. In those days, tenant farming was about the only way of life for black families in the rural South, and it was the only life Robert McRae knew in his early life. Most of these families just survived from year to year.

When World War II came along, Robert joined the army in 1943, and defended his country in the European theater, having served in France, England and Belgium. When Robert came home from the war, he came back to the same life he left. Things had not changed much for African Americans with regard to jobs and opportunity. He worked on the tobacco markets for a while, and his first full-time job was working at the Wilson Smith Veneer Company. Later he worked for the Truax Veneer Company. Robert married Teressa Dudley, and they have been together for sixty years.

When Dixiana Mills came to Dillon, Robert got a break and got on with the mill. He worked for Dixiana Mills for twenty-nine years and retired before the company closed.

Now we get to the amazing thing about Robert McRae's life. In order to supplement his income, he began driving a taxi part time. Robert began

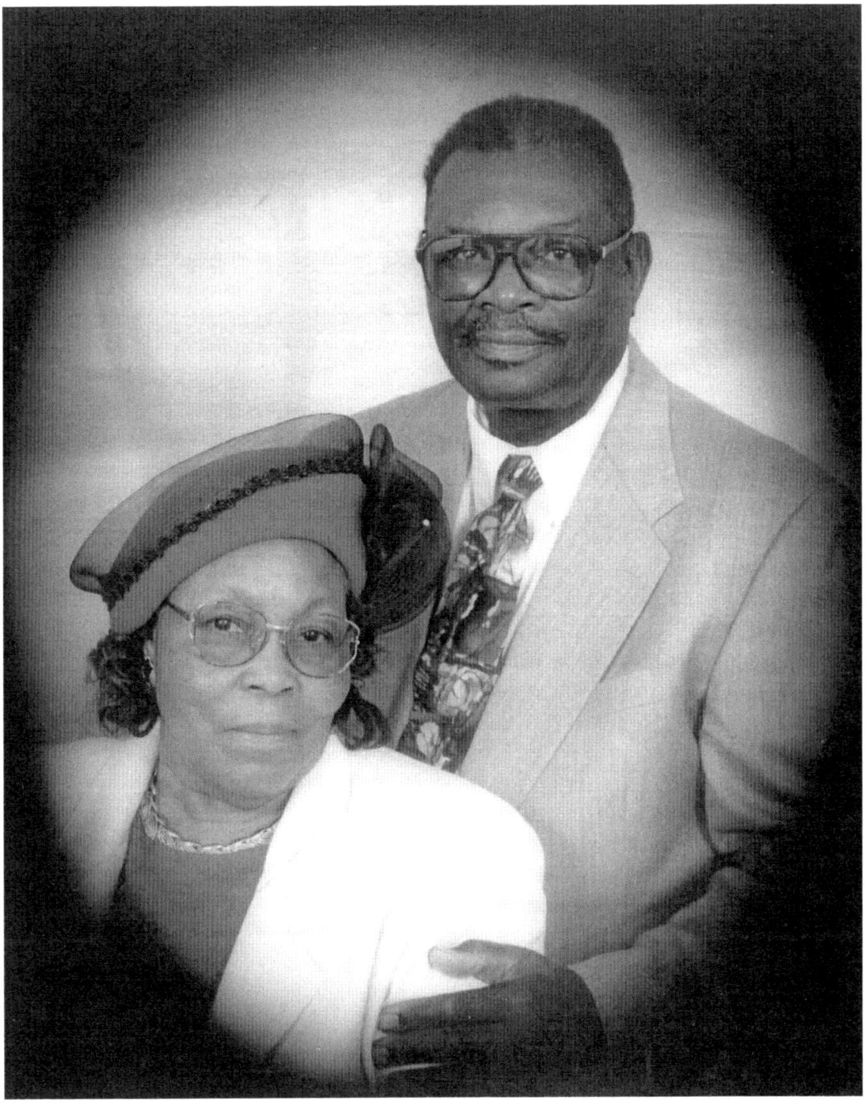

Mr. Robert and Teressa Dudley McRae. *Courtesy of Deloris McRae-Augustus.*

driving in 1953, some fifty-three years ago. He said his first cab was a 1950 Chevrolet. Since then he has gone through eight cars, and he still drives a Chevrolet—a 1988 model that looks like it just rolled off the showroom floor. When Mr. McRae began driving the taxi, there were twenty-three black drivers and just as many white drivers in Dillon. This was a time when every home didn't have two or three cars sitting in the yard. Robert said when he first started driving a cab, he would pick up a person from the grocery store and take them across town for fifty cents. You could go to Little Rock for a dollar and a half or go to Latta for two dollars. The price of gasoline then was thirty cents a gallon. Mr. McRae said he had taken fares to as far away as Walterboro, South Carolina, Fayetteville and Wilmington, North Carolina, but over the years, the need for taxi service has greatly declined.

Today, Dillon has seven thousand people and only one taxi, and that is the taxi of Robert McRae. Robert McRae, at the age of eighty-one, even though he looks about sixty and is still in good health, will take you where you need to go. Robert maintains a cab stand at 206 East Hampton Street in Dillon and his phone number is 774-9111. He doesn't drive on Sunday; that day he attends church at McCoy's Chapel United Methodist Church at Little Rock.

Robert says that sometimes he might not get a call in two hours, but it gives him something to do and many of the same customers have used him for years. He says the busiest time for him is around the first of the month when a lot of folks get their monthly checks. Robert proudly wears his cabdriver's cap, with his name plate on the front of the cap. Robert takes a lot of pride in what he does, and if I were in need of a cab, I would be proud to ride with Robert McRae.

Robert and Teressa McRae, who worked for Winn-Dixie for many years, have a nice home on Ninth Avenue and have been on that street longer than anyone else. The McRaes have raised a good family of six children: three boys and three girls. Their names are Raymond McRae, Deloris McRae-Augustus, Robert Lee McRae, Claretha Whitfield, Gloria Summerville and Edward Dewey McRae.

All children graduated high school, and Deloris and Clarethea went to Technical School. Gloria graduated from North Carolina Central University. Two of the daughters were present when I interviewed Mr. McRae, and as he spoke, I could see the admiration in their eyes for their parents. Folks, this is something you can't buy at Wal-Mart. This admiration is from years of living a life before your children that they can respect. The youngest son, Edward Dewey, retired from the U.S. Air Force, and Mr. McRae proudly showed me a fine Cadillac automobile under his carport that his son had given him. The McRaes also have twelve grandchildren, of whom four have graduated from college, and two great-grandchildren.

Robert McRae came up in a time when African Americans didn't have much chance in the rural South, but he took the cards that he was dealt and made the most of it, and I believe that life has been good for the McRae family. Robert McRae might not go down in the history books, but I believe

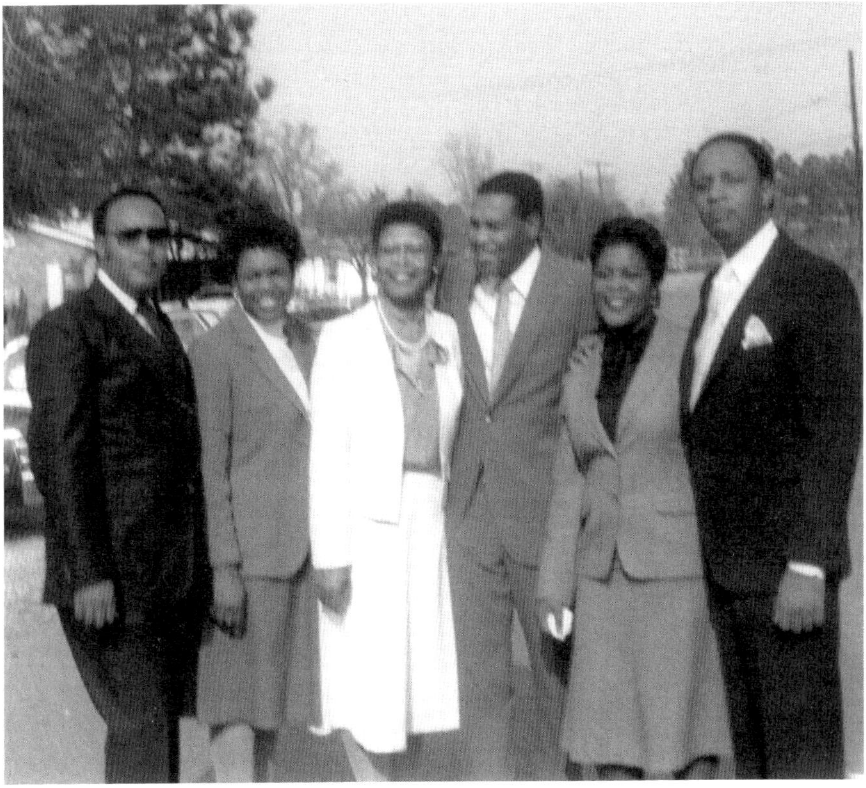

Raymond McRae, Deloris McRae-Augustus, Robert Lee McRae, Claretha Whitfield, Gloria Summerville and Edward Dewey McRae. *Courtesy of Robert McRae.*

that when he leaves this world, he will leave fond memories among family and friends. And how about all those people that Robert McRae has driven in his cabs over the fifty-three years that he has been in the taxi business? I asked him how long he intended to drive, and he said as long as he felt safe in what he was doing.

If you have never ridden in a taxi, why not call Robert McRae and take a ride? You could also say you rode with the Last Taxi Driver, perhaps the last this town will ever have. You will also get some good conversation from a very wise man. Robert said that in fifty-three years, he has heard every story in the book, but just how many were true he didn't know. When I wrote articles on downtown Dillon fifty years ago, I covered the white cabdrivers of that area. With the help of the McRae family, I would like to name the African American cabdrivers who have served the people of Dillon.

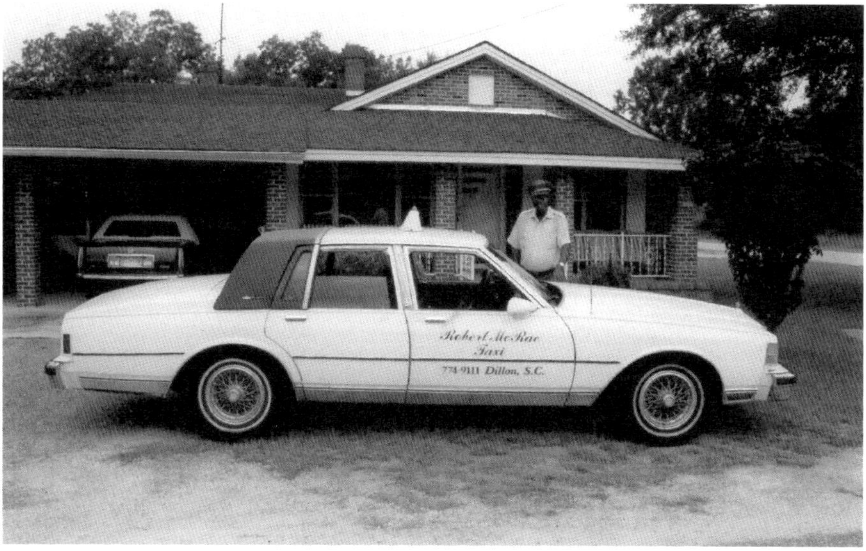

Mr. Robert McRae, the Last Taxi Driver. *Photo by Helen Wiggins.*

There was John C. Thomas, James Thomas, Frank Palmer, Frank Bethea, Jimmy Campbell, William Campbell, John Wesley Campbell, Mack Campbell, Willie Lee Cribb, Lawrence McEachearn, Jay McEachearn, Allen McEachearn, Oscar McNeil, Danny Griffin, Henry McLean, Make McRae, Hang Nance, Robert Dudley, Willie Bethea, Willie Maxwell, Uler C. Vanderhall, Clarence Thomas, Lindsey Campbell, Leo Smith, Levi McGill, the Manning Taxis and Marshall Campbell, who now runs a limousine service. And don't forget Dillon's Last Taxi Driver: Mr. Robert McRae, one of Dillon County's finest citizens.

There is a footnote to this story that I wrote two years ago. Just a few days ago, I saw in the paper a nice ad that Robert McRae had placed announcing that he was retiring from the taxi business on May, 31, 2008. He thanked all the people that had used his service over the years. I guess after fifty-five years, he deserves to sit on his porch and enjoy the rest of his days. Robert McRae has called it quits at the age of eighty-three. Dillon's Last Taxi Driver has parked his cab and hung up his cap.

SLIM MIMS—FROM THE COTTON MILL TO HOLLYWOOD

Since I began writing articles that are published in the local newspaper some time back, I have wanted to write about a man that I followed most of my life, a man that was a household word in this part of the country. That man was the late Slim Mims.

Even though I remembered as a small boy seeing Slim and his band at country schools such as Bingham and New Holly, Dillon County, South Carolina, listening to him on the radio and seeing him on TV for many years, I still did not know a lot about him. So I called his sister, Mrs. Floyd (Margie) Griffin, who still lives in this area. When I told her what I had in mind, she replied, "Carley, I will tell you what I know, but I don't know how much I can help you."

We set a time for me to go by and see her, and when I got there, she had stacks of newspaper articles, old programs from his shows and many old pictures of his bands, as well as a very impressive video that was made after his death. She had saved this precious material throughout his career. When she referred to him as Charles, it was the first time that I had ever heard his real name.

Charles Edward Mims was born in Columbia, South Carolina, the son of Charlie Thomas and Katie Owens Mims, on July 9, 1918. When he was a boy, the family moved to the small community of Hamer, Dillon County, where the Mims family operated a store on the grounds of the Hamer Spinning Mill, Dillon County's oldest industry. Slim was the oldest child of the Mims children, with a brother Brown Mims and the only surviving child, Mrs. Margie Griffin. Slim's family always called him by his given name, Charles. He came by the name Slim because he was tall and slim in stature.

His desire to make music developed in the shadow of a cotton mill. Plunking on a guitar was the only way to escape the roar of the textile machines. Music overtook this lad of fourteen and would become his life forever.

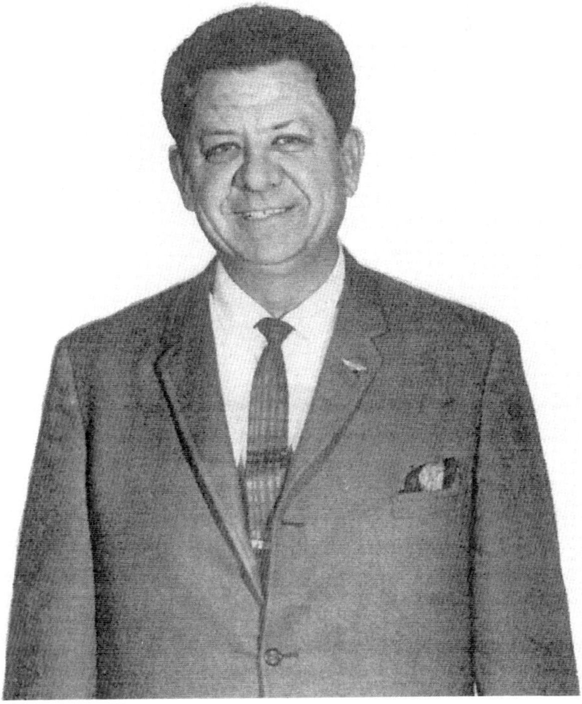

Charles Edward "Slim" Mims. *Courtesy of Marjorie Mims Griffin.*

During the eighth grade, he dropped out of school to help the Mims family make a living. Things were very hard back then, as the country was trying to recover from the Great Depression. Slim said the last year he went to school, he had one pair of pants, and holes came in them during the year. His mother dyed patches from a sheet to cover the holes.

He began to work in the mill at night and in the family store during the day. Some of the mill hands would come by the store during slack hours, and they would play a few tunes. Mrs. Griffin said she remembered J.R. Wilson, who drove the Merita bread truck, would come by the store and show Slim a few chords on the guitar. I remembered J.R. as well; he was a super nice fellow. Slim saved his money and bought a fifty-dollar music course and an eleven-dollar guitar and walked six miles to Dillon each Saturday to take the course.

The Hawaiian Harmonizers was the name of the first band Slim had, which consisted of Bobby Graham, "Pud" Adams, Pearl Adams, Tom Adams and Slim. The band decided to save fifty dollars each and "hit the road." They landed in Kinston, North Carolina. They had a morning radio show on the local radio station, and after the radio show, Slim would go out to try to find bookings for places where the band could play.

The five stayed in an attic room at the Queen Street Inn. With little money coming in, they had to cut down on food. One of the band members would go to the local bakery each day and buy day-old cinnamon buns, which they would soak overnight in the sink. When the landlady found out that the band had no food, she would let them come downstairs at night after everyone had gone and eat what was left.

Slim was eighteen years old at the time. They were playing to school audiences, pocketing as little as twelve dollars on one night. Then the final straw broke. One night the transmission in the old Chevy fell out and it took every cent they had to get it fixed and get back to Kinston.

The band headed home. He shoved his guitar under the bed and it stayed there for a year. Slim was a pretty fair baseball player and he played in the Piedmont League, making fifteen to twenty dollars for playing on Sundays. In 1940, while he was driving to Dillon, he picked up Bill Strickland, who told him that a band in Fayetteville, North Carolina, the Oklahoma Sweethearts, was looking for a business manager, someone who knew the ropes and knew how to get bookings. Slim went to Fayetteville to manage the band and shortly after changed the band's name to the Dream Ranch Boys. This name would stick with him throughout his musical career.

They played around Fayetteville until 1944, when Uncle Sam came calling for Slim—his career was put on hold when he was drafted into the U.S. Navy. He remained in the navy until January of 1946, and was discharged with the rank of quartermaster second class. His sister, Margie Griffin, said that Slim spent a lot of his time in the navy entertaining the troops aboard his ship with his musical talents.

During his time in the navy, he gave a lot of thought to giving up the music business for something more stable. He thought about becoming a textile designer, but not long after Slim arrived back home, he began to get calls to play with one combo or another. In a few months, the Dream Ranch Boys were back in business.

The Dillon radio station, WDSC, opened about that time and Slim and his band opened the station every day at noon. By the second week, the mail was pouring in, sometimes a sack at a time. The personal appearances were coming in and Slim worked hard with the band, blending them to the sound that twenty years ago had been too advanced. They stayed in Dillon fourteen months and then moved to Florence to a new station, WJMX, where he remained for twenty years. During his early years in Florence, he developed his "Uncle Ugly" personality, which was a great addition to the show. As a band

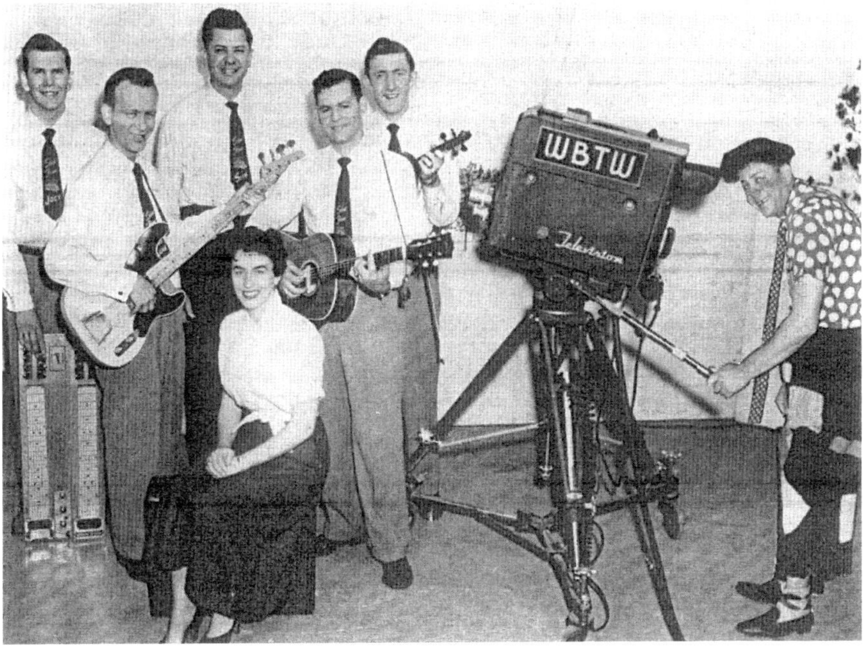

Slim Mims and the Dream Ranch Boys. *Courtesy of Marjorie Mims Griffin.*

leader, he was a composed, stately man. As "Uncle Ugly," he was cornball antics in a clown costume. I remember Slim as he would portray the "Uncle Ugly" character. He would bring a lot of laughs from those who watched with the silly looking clothes, a flop hat and a tie that reached the floor. He would paint his face with black dots and missing teeth and speak in a high pitched voice. It was hard to believe that the two were the same person.

About 1948, the Dream Ranch Boys went from playing for $15 a night to $200 a night. Things were really looking up for the band. Now they had a nice Cadillac to ride in to their personal appearances. Slim always did have a nice car to drive. He and his band still had time for other matters, such as the time they made a detour to stage a surprise birthday party for Slim's mom on her sixtieth birthday.

In 1953, under unusual circumstances, the band took on a female vocalist, Patricia Fay Cooper, who about a year later would become Slim's second wife and a part of his life for the rest of his days. On the show, she was known as Patti Fay. He and Patricia had two children. Slim's first wife was Juanita English, and they had five children. Slim Mims had become a multitalented man. He was not only a good band leader. He was a very funny comedian,

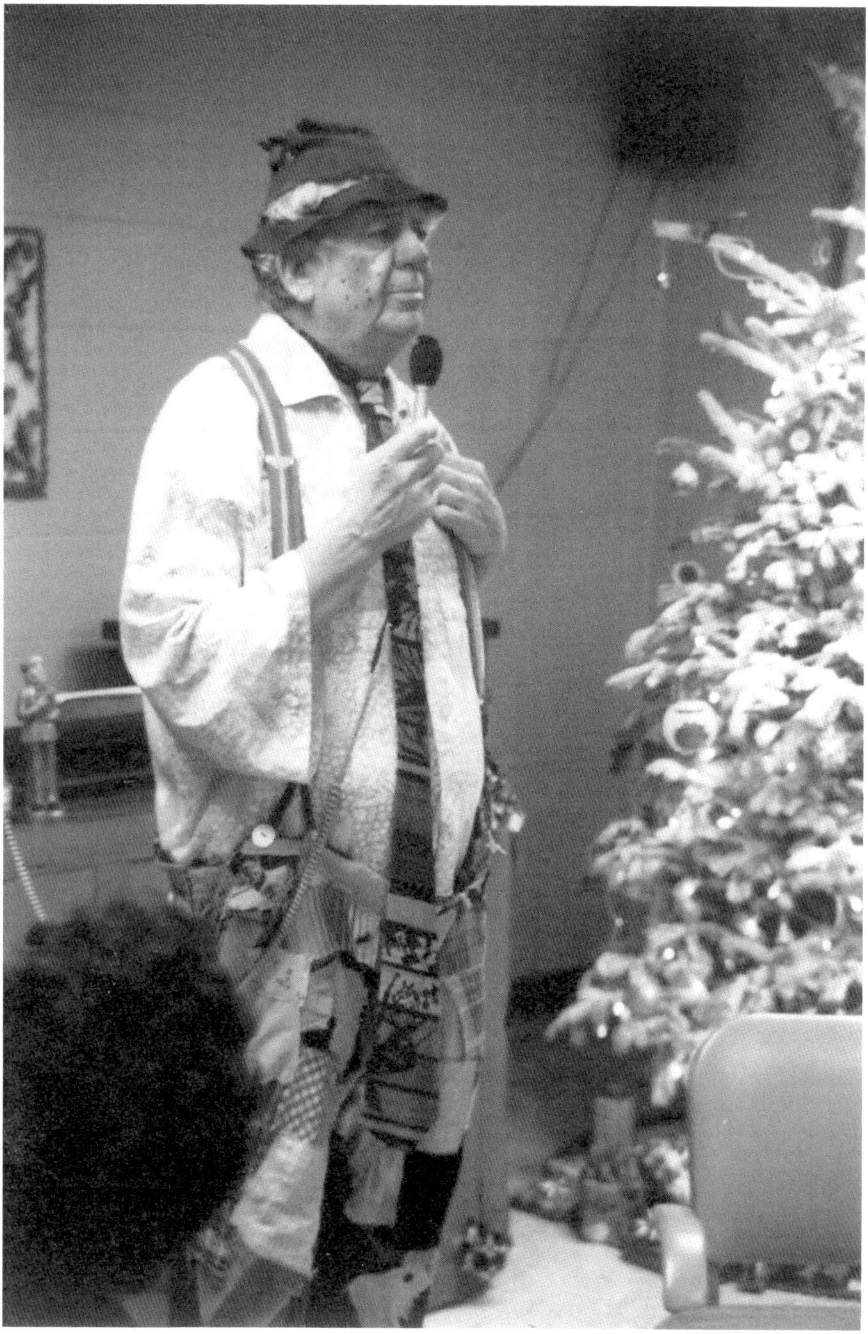

Slim Mims as "Uncle Ugly." *Courtesy of Marjorie Mims Griffin.*

as the "Uncle Ugly" character, singing "Slap her down again Paw." He was known to play several musical instruments, but was best known for the steel guitar and another instrument called the dobro.

Slim went on to be a very popular television personality. He started his TV career with WBTW in Florence when it was still Channel 8. I don't know just how many years he was at the station, but I know it was a long time. At one time, he had a Sunday morning show called *Hymns from the Hills*, and Monday through Friday, the *Slim Mims Show* started the morning with an hour production. During this time, he also had the radio show as well as many other things going on. He was a very busy man.

It would be impossible to mention all the people who played with Slim over the years, but I am sure that you will remember some of these names. In the early days, I remember a fiddler named J.Q. Parker who lived in Dillon. I have photos of some of his early band members, but I cannot recall some of their names. I remember a comic named "Greasy" Medlin, but I never knew what his real name was. There was Jodi Joiner, Billie Kiker, Danny Ray, Ira Ford, Buck Wade, Lew Price, "Little Joe" Black, Luke Spivey, Lacy Richardson and Jim Nesbitt, and I remember a young man named Russ Hicks, who was a very talented performer and who, I am told, went on to play on the *Grand Ole Opry* and also performed on *Hee Haw* for a good while. Slim Mims and his Dream Ranch Boys were without a doubt the most popular group to come from this area.

While talking to Patti Faye Mims, Slim's widow, I discovered that while he performed on WBTW that they rented an abandoned building in Florence, South Carolina, and made a country music theater out of it. They had many big-name country stars on the show, such as Kitty Wells, Carl Smith and Ernest Tubb, just to name a few. On Wednesday night, they would also have wrestling matches. I also learned that Slim and his band had opened shows for some great superstars, such as Hank Williams Sr. and Waylon Jennings.

Among other great talents, he later became an excellent photographer. He was a ham operator for many years, but one of his greatest skills, other than music, was as a pilot. He owned several planes and became a commercial pilot and opened his own charter service. His plane would charter people to some of the larger airports. Some of his customers were Clint Eastwood, "Elly May" of *Beverly Hillbillies* fame and Frog Millhouse, who played in many movies.

While playing a show at the pavilion in Myrtle Beach, Slim was discovered by a well-known agent, who wanted Slim to go to New York. Slim went to New York and was made a great offer, but he declined because it would keep him too far from his family. Slim was very devoted to his family and wanted to stay close to his mother.

In 1968, cosmetics millionaire Glenn Turner convinced Slim to move to Florida and join his cosmetics business. Slim and his family moved to Florida and had the finest of everything, but after two years, Slim missed the Pee Dee area, so they moved back to Florence. There he went into the insurance business, but Slim was a showman, and he missed the entertainment business. WECT TV in Wilmington, North Carolina, called and offered him an hour-long morning show on Channel 6, so Slim and his family moved to Wilmington and stayed there for four years. Then he went back to his first love, which was radio. He had a show on a station in Lumberton, North Carolina, and a Sunday morning show on WOLS in Florence.

During his fifteen-year stay on WBTW TV in Florence, he was selected to go to Hollywood to do a picture session with the stars of the *Beverly Hillbillies* and *Petticoat Junction*. Then in 1974, he made it to the big screen to play the part of Slim Mims and his Jamboree in a Columbia Pictures movie called *Buster and Billie*.

His career spanned over fifty years in a business that he loved dearly. He was known as a man that everybody liked, and he was so very talented. I can hear him now, playing the "Steel Guitar Rag."

Charles Edward "Slim" Mims departed this life fourteen years ago on February 13, 1994, at the age of seventy-six. His body rests at Riverside Cemetery in Dillon near his parents and Pattie Faye. She passed away at age seventy-two on April 27, 2007, in Dillon, South Carolina.

I hope that Slim Mims will never be forgotten, because he brought so much joy and entertainment to so many lives. My special thanks to the people who made this story possible: his sister Margie Griffin; the family of Billy Kiker, a member of Slim's band that is still living near Atlanta, Georgia; and his wife of forty-two years, Patti Faye Mims. Slim said he could not have made it without her.

Slim Mims was perhaps the most popular entertainer to come from Dillon County. He was known as a fine person who took time to spend with friends and fans, whom he loved. A lot of people still remember Slim Mims, and when the name comes up, he is talked about with dignity and respect. Even though Slim never made it to the top of the music industry, his talent and musical ability along with his sparkling personality made him a star with the people in this area.

MASON LEE—INSANE OR GENIUS?

This story is about one of the strangest individuals to ever live in the Pee Dee area or anywhere else as far as that is concerned. I began to research this man about nine months ago, mostly because his sister, Sally Lee, married a Wiggins. Mason Lee was born in the year 1770 in Martin County, North Carolina. He was apparently born to a very normal family with some wealth because by adulthood he had become an accountant. For the first thirty years of his life, he seemed to be a very normal person, but one day during a violent thunderstorm, he was struck by lighting and that apparently changed Mason Lee's life forever.

Soon after the accident, he moved to Washington County, Georgia. While in Georgia, he killed a man, and I don't know all the details but, fearing prosecution, he fled the area and settled on the Great Pee Dee River near Brownsville in what is now Marlboro County. The first time I find him purchasing land was in 1808, when he bought fifty acres on the Pee Dee River. While in this area, he would live a strange, dark and haunted life.

Almost everyone thought he was crazy, but a few considered him merely eccentric. As he began to buy land and build a plantation, his ways became more and more erratic. He walked into a livery stable and asked the owner about a certain horse. They agreed on a price, and Lee paid the man, then pulled out a knife and cut the horse's ears and tail off. He treated all his animals like that; he said it would make them poor if they spent all their time swatting flies with their tails and ears.

Mason Lee lived the most frugal life possible. The saddle for his horse was made from a hollow gum log covered with leather, and the reins and stirrups were made from grapevines. Even though he apparently made a lot of money, he lived in a very small, one-room house, not nearly as good as the workers on his farm lived in. The door to his house was so small that he would have to bend over to enter the house. The stables were built around the house with the pig pen directly in front of the house. His bed was also a hollow gum log, which is on display in the Marlboro County Museum today. The only other furniture in his house was a trunk that also served as the table where he would eat. He ate only boar and bull meat cooked with dumplings that were served up in the same pot that he cooked the food in. He owned no forks or spoons, so he ate with a forked stick. Lee made his own clothes, which had no buttons. His pants were as wide as petticoats, and his coat was a blanket with a hole cut for his head to go through. Those who knew him said he would go for months without washing his clothes.

Mason Lee never married, but sometime while in this area, he had an affair with an unknown woman, who bore him a set of twins. They went by the name of Penniwell. One of the sons he claimed, but the other he would not claim. He said it was because one boy would crawl under a fence while the other would climb over it.

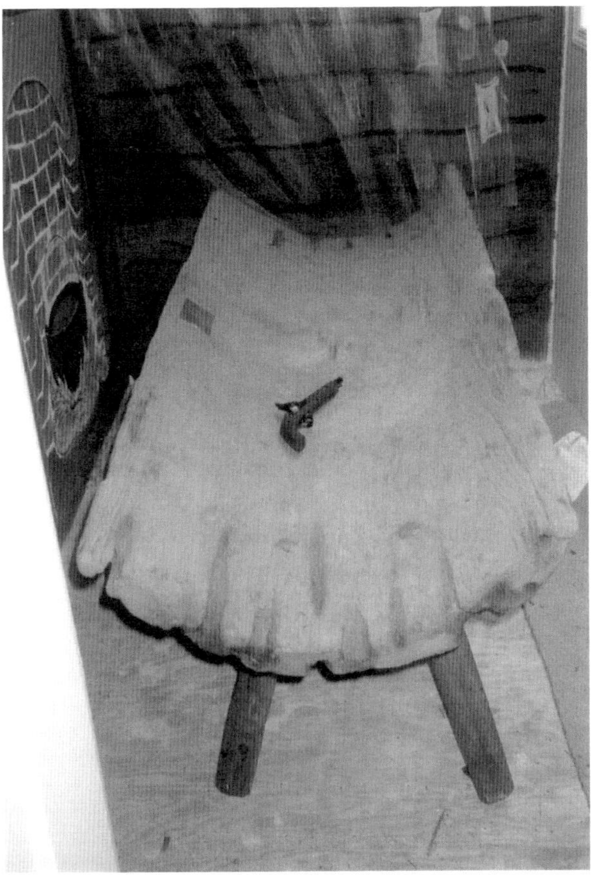

The bed of Mason Lee.
Photo by Helen L. Wiggins.

Lee became obsessed with spirits and demons. He would not allow any woman to enter or clean his house because he thought all women were witches. He owned fourteen custom-made swords that he used to fight off the spirits. Some of them had blades as wide as fourteen inches. At night, he could be heard striking and thrashing about his house, trying to fight off the spirits. Sometimes, he would summon his workers to throw dirt on his house to drive the spirits away. His hat had a hole on each side; he said if the devil came in one side, he could drive him out the other side.

Lee would cut the quarters off his shoes, so if the devil got in his feet, he could kick him out. He believed that his closest relatives, the Wiggins family, were trying to cast spells on him, and that they had become lodged in his teeth. He extracted fourteen good teeth to get the Wiggins out of his teeth—he felt that the Wiggins were out to get his money, and also trying to return him to Georgia for the crime he had committed.

Most people felt Lee was a poor businessman. He would have plows made in odd shapes that were impossible to work with, and he bought a thousand acres of land to plant peanuts on, but never planted the first acre. He sold a man a parcel of land for $7,000, and gave the man seventeen years to pay the money back with the agreement that if the man was not satisfied, he would owe him nothing. He would hoe his corn after frost in the belief that it would come back again.

Sometime before his death, Lee went to live with a Mr. Dubose in Darlington County. Lee was so filthy that Dubose would not let him live in his house, so Lee told him to build him a house in the yard, five feet long by three feet wide and four feet high. This is where Mason Lee lived out his life. Mason Lee died in 1820, at the age of fifty.

Mason Lee's strangeness even followed him to the grave. Before he died, he designed his own coffin, made like a seaman's chest. Mason Lee is buried at the old Brownsville Cemetery, now known as Rogers's Cemetery. I visited Lee's grave, which is located away from the other graves in the cemetery, and it is one of the strangest graves I have ever seen. It was constructed of brick and arranged in a V shape. Standing beside the grave, I felt a little eerie. Maybe he is still after the Wiggins.

Mason Lee only lived fifty years total and only twelve years in this area, but he left a legacy that most historians will never forget. People considered him a lunatic, but when he died, he owned nineteen thousand acres in four counties with a net value of over $50,000. That would amount to a fortune in this time. Many prominent people in Bennettsville borrowed money from him at times. A lot of people who knew him considered him crazy, but was he crazy or was he a pure genius?

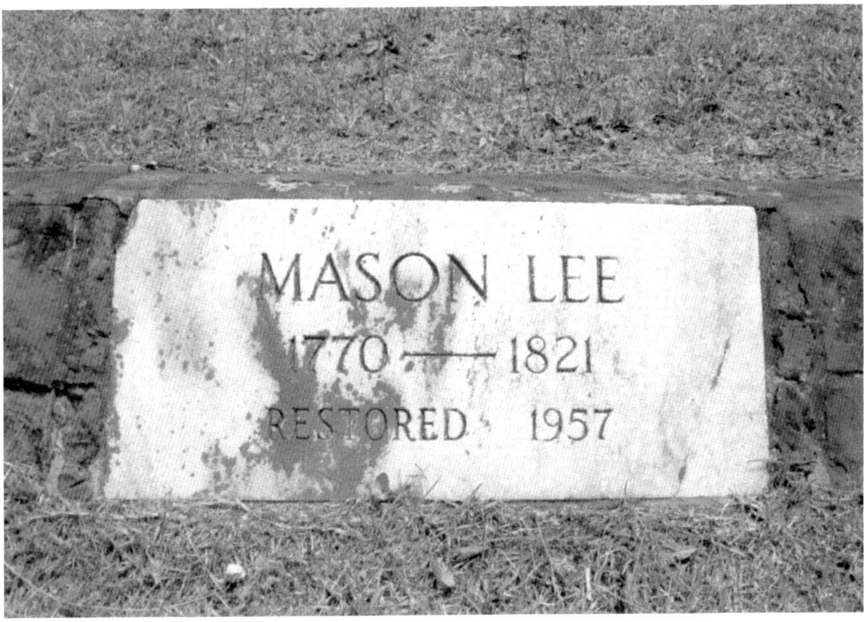

Mason Lee's grave. *Photo by Helen L. Wiggins.*

Now we come to the part that Mason Lee is most remembered for, and that was the writing of a most controversial will the same year that he died, 1820. This will has been studied around the world in colleges and universities for nearly two hundred years.

As I have mentioned, Lee thought that his relatives were out to get his money. His closest relatives were the Wiggins and Taylor families, whom he distrusted very much. When Lee wrote his will some months before his death, he left his vast estate to the State of South Carolina and the State of Tennessee. He left each state an equal share and did not leave his heirs one penny. Oddly enough, he did not know anyone from Tennessee and had never even been to that state.

Lee appointed Roberson Carloss, an attorney from Bennettsville, to be his executor, and in the will he stated that "as long as trees grow and rivers run," no member of the Wiggins family was to ever get any of his money. He instructed Carloss to hire the finest lawyers in Charleston to protect his wishes. His wishes were carried out as instructed.

Enter one Baker Wiggins, a nephew of Mason Lee who had also moved from Martin County, North Carolina, and had settled in the Great Pee Dee area. He had bought land in the area now known as Pee Dee and also in the Mars Bluff area. His mother was Mason Lee's sister. Born in 1777, Baker Wiggins was an educated man and had become prominent and well regarded since moving to South Carolina. I found many old documents that Wiggins had signed in land transactions and other business matters. Wiggins became a successful land owner and acquired a good-sized estate himself. There is a landing on the Pee Dee called Wiggins Landing, which was named for him. Baker Wiggins, on behalf of the heirs of Mason Lee, challenged Lee's will on the grounds of his mental capacity. D.D. McColl, in his book, *The Sketches of Old Marlboro*, had much to say about this strange individual and his celebrated will.

The case was first heard before Ordinary (judge) William Easterling on June 23, 1823. The case was adjourned to the new Marlboro County Courthouse, which was moved from the river to downtown Bennettsville. This was the first case to be tried in the new courthouse. The new trial was heard before Judge Thomas Waits. A jury trial was held, and Samuel Gillespie served as foreman of the jury.

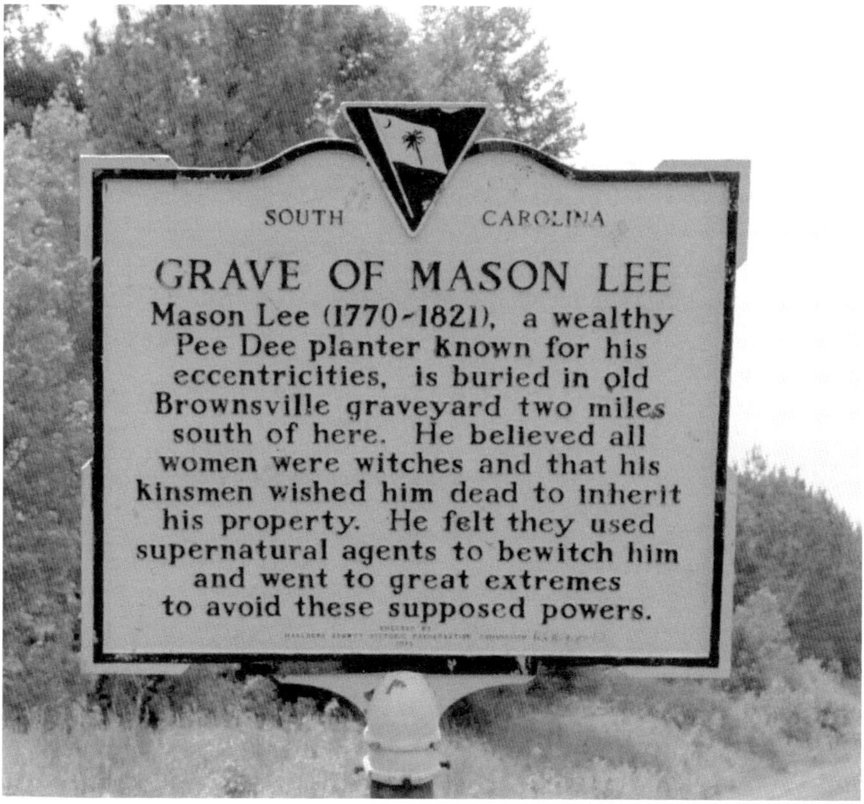

Mason Lee historical marker. *Photo by Helen L. Wiggins.*

The decision before the court was whether Lee was of sound mind when the will was written. Many witnesses were called to testify for and against the strange will. The jury found that even though Lee was apparently deranged at certain times, he could also make sound decisions at other times.

The jury upheld Lee's will, but the heirs of Mason Lee appealed the verdict to the state Supreme Court. The state's highest court upheld the decision, and the will stood as written. A short while later, Lee's executor Roberson Carloss died, and a new executor was appointed. Then in 1829, James R. Ervin, a lawyer who had represented the heirs in the earlier trials and who was also a state senator, introduced legislation in the state senate to set aside the controversial will and award the heirs what was rightly theirs.

The bill was passed, and the state awarded one half of the South Carolina inheritance to the heirs of Mason Lee and one half to the South Carolina Mental Hospital. It is not known what happened to the portion that was left to the State of Tennessee.

Baker Wiggins passed away in 1829, and his son Ricks B. Wiggins was named executor of the estate. Due to litigation expenses and wastefulness by the final executor, the estate was soon gone. The famous estate fell into the hands of Robert Campbell, a congressman from Marlboro County. Baker Wiggins had five children, all of whom moved away from South Carolina. Ricks B. Wiggins moved to Arkansas and died in 1831.

This famous case was contested in the courts for nearly ten years. Mason Lee's strange wishes were carried out after all. None of his relations enjoyed any of his money, and this case is still taught to law students today about mental capacity in a court of law.

I would like to point out that the Baker Wiggins mentioned in this story is not related to this writer, and as far as I can tell is not related to another Baker Wiggins who lived in the Wahee community of Marion County in the 1800s.

HATCH'S LUNCH

Every now and then I get to thinking about old times and places around Dillon and the surrounding area, and a certain place will come across my mind, and I will try and put the place together and just what it looked like and where it was located. Just a few days back, I got to thinking about a place that brought back some fond memories to me.

That place was Hatch's Lunch, and it was started by Mr. Clyde Hatch and his wife, whom I only knew as Mrs. Hatch. Hatch's Lunch was on Main Street in Dillon in the vicinity of where King's Pizza is now located. I don't know exactly when the small diner opened, but I would say sometime in the 1930s. I remember some people that were about ten years older than me saying they used to buy six hot dogs for a quarter at Hatch's Lunch.

The building was not much to look at as I recall; it was made of tin siding and the roof was very low. I became familiar with Hatch's Lunch in the mid-fifties, when I started going there to buy sandwiches. Mr. Clyde Hatch was already deceased by this time, and Mrs. Hatch and her son Jack operated the place. Mrs. Hatch was a very pleasant woman with a nice smile and the prettiest silver hair I think I ever saw. Jack was a quiet fellow, slim in stature and over six feet tall. Jack was a little hard of hearing; I remember him putting his hand to his ear in order to hear better what you were saying.

When you walked in the door, there was a large glass counter on the right that looked like maybe it was a candy counter at one time. Behind the counter was the grill where the hot dogs, hamburgers and other sandwiches were prepared. On the left were maybe five small tables with chairs where you could sit down and eat your food if you desired. Mrs. Hatch cooked plate lunches at noontime, and a regular crowd that would come in to have her daily special. She only had one choice of meat per day, but everything she cooked was good. I remember she made some very good beef stew, cut into small cubes, which were always tender. You could get a heaping plate of the beef stew and gravy served over rice for seventy-five cents.

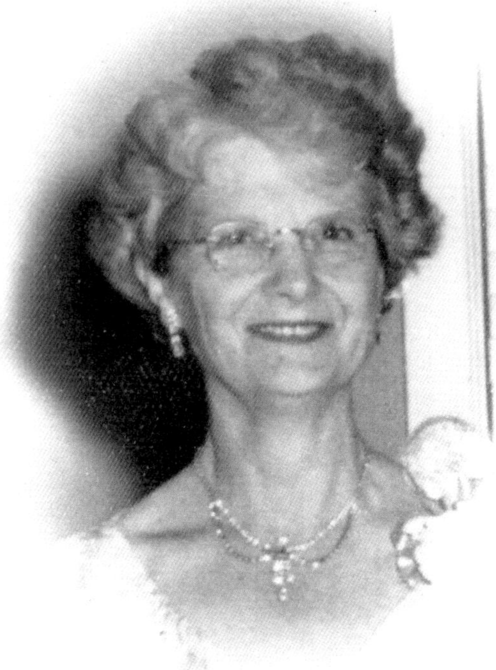

Mrs. Clyde Hatch. *Courtesy of Lura H. Hinnant.*

Jack handled most of the sandwiches; he was the first person I saw that grilled his hot dogs. He would grill the wieners and toast the buns. He didn't have chili; he just put mustard and ketchup on the hot dogs, but they were as good as any that I have eaten at any place. The price was fifteen cents each. I could buy two hot dogs and a large bottle drink for forty cents. He also made a ten-cent hamburger that consisted of a beef patty and two pieces of loaf bread. You could buy a large bag of these tasty hamburgers for a dollar.

Jack was a tall man, and the building had a dip about halfway back, and Jack knew exactly where to duck his head to keep from banging his head on the wooden beam. I guess he ran into that beam many times before he remembered where it was.

I think the thing that I enjoyed most about Hatch's Lunch was the roast pork sandwiches that Mrs. Hatch made. They were made with real baked ham, lettuce and tomato. They were not like the fast-food sandwiches that you might find today; the ham was a generous portion that you could really get your teeth into. The cost was thirty-five cents.

In the late 1960s, the entire block where the diner was located was bought by the Atkinson family from Latta, and the A&P store was built on the back of

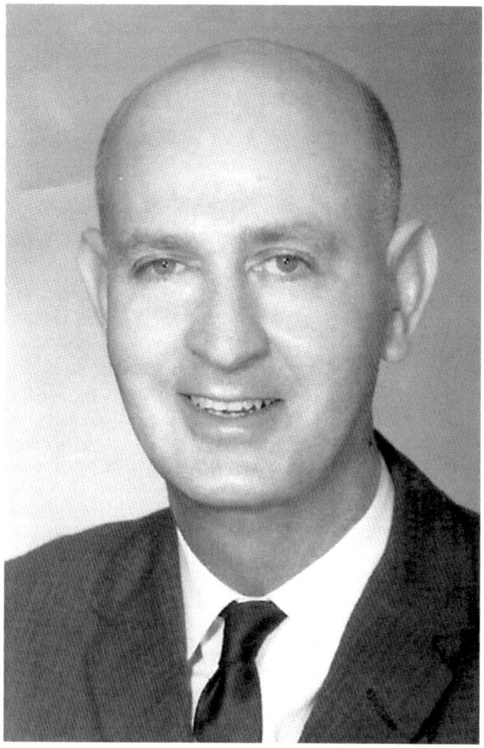

Jack Hatch. *Courtesy of Lura H. Hinnant.*

the lot, which today is the Family Dollar store. Several of the other buildings were torn down to build more modern structures. Hatch's Lunch was also one of the buildings to go. Mrs. Hatch retired and passed away some years later. Jack, who had a degree in accounting but had stayed with his mother at the diner all those years to help her out, went to work at the auditor's office.

He was elected as Dillon County Auditor for one term but was defeated in his second try for the office. Jack was a good accountant, but not a politician. He continued to work for the auditor's office until his retirement. It is common knowledge among Dillon's older citizens that Jack was the one of the best ever to work in our auditor's office. Late at night, you could see the light on in the auditor's office; Jack Hatch was the last person to leave the building at night.

When Hatch's Lunch closed, another little piece of Dillon history was gone. I doubt the old building would meet the building codes of today, but a lot of good food was served there. I remember Mrs. Hatch's silver hair and her pleasant personality, and the pretty aprons she would wear. I sure wish I had one of those roast pork sandwiches about now. While I was working on this article, I thought how good it would be if I had a picture of the old diner.

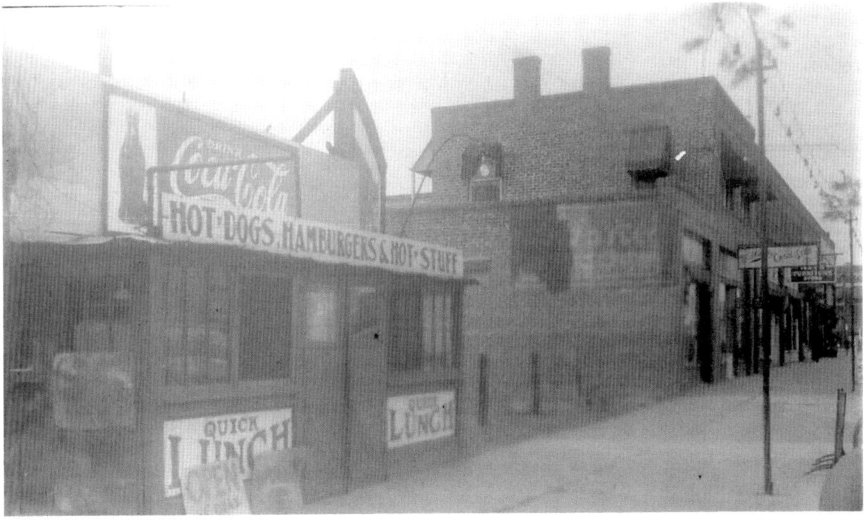

Hatch's Lunch. *Courtesy of Lura H. Hinnant.*

While talking with my stepdaughter, Lisa Gray, who works for the Dillon County Council, she said that Jack Hatch was still living. Lisa got some phone numbers for us, and we found that Jack was in a nursing home in Columbia. We also found out that he had a sister, Lura, whom I didn't even know about, that lives in Columbia also. We gave her a call, and I told her what I was doing and asked if she had a picture of the old diner. I was elated when she said, "Why yes, I do have a picture of the old place." She sent us the picture and the article was published the following week.

We sent copies of the article to Lura and she carried a copy to the nursing home and put it on the wall in Jack's room. Jack was in critical condition at this time and was unable to speak, but his sister said that he would look at the picture of the diner and a smile would come across his face. A short time thereafter, on June 5, 2006, Jack Hatch passed away. He was eighty-four years old.

When Jack passed away, his body was returned to Dillon to be buried at Riverside Cemetery with his mother and father. Jack had never married. A small service was held at the cemetery, and I guess about twenty-five people attended, mostly what little family he had and some folks who remembered him from when he worked with county. His sister Lura told us at the graveside how much she appreciated the newspaper article because she could not believe anyone would even care about the old diner.

Jack Hatch will not go down in history as a famous person. He was a meek and shy man, but for those who knew him, he will be remembered for the years he sacrificed to help his mother at the little diner known as Hatch's Lunch.

IN SEARCH OF THE BINGHAM LIGHT

The story you are about to read is one that several people have asked me to write, but I really didn't have very much knowledge about the so-called light, and since I am not very interested in "ghost stories," I just put it off. Some things have come about recently that have persuaded me to do some research and try and write something on the fabled light.

Let me say right up front that this writer does not believe in witches, goblins or ghosts. I do believe, however, that there are unexplained things that no one has been able to find an answer for, but I don't believe they have anything to do with the supernatural. For example, I lived in a house in Dillon for twenty-two years where I heard some strange noises and would find doors open that had been closed, and hear knocks on the front or back door but no one was there. When I moved from there, these things were still happening, and I am not saying that it didn't puzzle or concern me, but I never sat up at night and worried about it or entertained the idea that the house was haunted. My son, who is now forty years old, still vows that the house was haunted.

The Bingham Light is a story that has been told for years. I was born and reared some five miles from Bingham, but I don't recall hearing very much about it until the 1970s. I have heard the story tossed back and forth for about forty years now, and I have heard so many different versions of the story that none of it made any sense. I never had a real desire to go and see what everybody what talking about. When I decided to research this story, I went to the Internet, where several sites talk about the light, and a local message board had a thread about the light several weeks back. I don't put a lot of stock in people who do not use their real names. I am convinced that a lot of this stuff is exaggerated and blown up to make it sound scarier than it really is.

I decided to seek out some real people with real names to talk to about the light, and who better than people who live and have lived in the area for many years? I ran into Elbert Cox, a fellow who was raised in the Bingham area, and asked him what his feeling was about the light. Elbert said that he had hunted all over the woods around Bingham and had not seen such a light, but he went on to say that he wasn't looking for a light and didn't believe any of the stories anyway.

I talked to Randall Coleman, a local businessman and an avid hunter who is a native of that community, and Randall was quick to respond, "Yes I have seen the Bingham Light many times." He said the first time he saw the light, he had never heard of it, and his biggest concern was to find out just what it was. He said after that he has witnessed the light several times; he even took friends and young people to witness the sight. Coleman said on one occasion he took two friends, Paul Gaddy and Todd Tribble, to the site, and the thing seemed to be angered and actually ran them out of the swamp. He said the light would move from place to place and it looked at one time like it was going to get into their truck.

I also talked to Ray Coleman Jr., who is Randall's older brother and a farmer in that area, and he said that he first witnessed the light back in the 1980s and has seen it many times since, along with other people he has taken there. Ray said he hunted these woods for years and that the light would usually appear around 3:30 a.m. He said that the light would never vary more than a hundred yards from one place and would always be about head high or about the height of a man carrying a lantern.

Both brothers told of a group of college students that they found in the swamp early one morning. The students were from a school for the deaf from out of state. They had gotten bogged down and had been there all night. They all were muddy and dirty; Ray pulled their car out with a tractor and took them to his house to clean up. He said later that he received a paper that they had written on the light and sent to him.

Before I go any further, for the benefit of you who have never heard of the Bingham Light, let me give you what history as I know it about the "mysterious light." Keep in mind that none of this is documented, and I have heard many stories, so I will give you the one that I have heard the most about. I have no idea how far back this goes or when it began, but supposedly there was a man named Bingham—some call him John and some Bill. It was said that the man drank a lot of moonshine liquor, and his mind had gotten bad. Another story said he killed his wife and children, so believe whatever you like.

The Short Line Railroad ran through Bingham at that time, and the man, supposedly in a drunken stupor, went to this spot where the light is now seen and laid his head on the tracks, and the train came along and cut off his head. The Bingham Light is supposed to be this fellow still looking for his head and the light is a lantern he is using to find it.

Ray Coleman gave another account that he had heard from some older people from around Bingham. He said the man's name was Joe Baldwin, and he was killed in a train wreck in that area. Let me point out that neither of the Coleman brothers is calling this a ghost. They simply don't know where it comes from. I have heard accounts of how the light looks; most say it is a glowing light much like a lantern might make; others say that it will change colors from green to red. Some say they have seen it in the tree tops, and others say it will appear in front of them and when they turn around, it will be behind them. Keep in mind that I am not writing this to prove or disprove anyone's story; I am simply telling what I have been told.

I talked to Jimmy Berry, a fellow about my age that I was in school with. Jimmy lived a good portion of his life just a short ways from the vicinity of the light, and, like Elbert Cox, said he never saw such a light. He said when this Bingham Light became so popular back in the seventies and eighties that it was more of a nuisance to him than anything else. Jimmy said that throngs of people would flood to the area to see the light and drive over his wheat fields and tear up his crops. He said that it got so bad that he had to put up a fence, but then they would take it down to get to the site.

He said that at one time it got so bad that he would have to go down there at night to keep the sightseers off his property. He remembered times when carloads of people would go there and drink and curse at the light to come out. On one occasion, he said they took a band down to the site and played music while waiting for the light. He said many times late at night, people would knock at his door and ask, "Would you come and pull us out of a bog?" He said after a few times, the first thing he would ask is, "How much money do you have in your pocket?" As I talked to Jimmy about the light, I told him that I planned to write an article on the light and I needed someone to take me to the location and maybe tell me what they had heard or seen concerning it. At the time I talked to Jimmy, he had left the farm several years ago and moved to Latta. He told me that since then he had never really seen the light and that a young man named Chad Garris who rented his farmhouse would be the best man to talk to, because he was an avid hunter and could probably help me more than anyone else.

I called Chad, who installs custom-made doors, mostly for industrial and storage buildings. Chad said he would be happy to talk with me and would even take me to the site where the light appears. We set a time to meet at Chad's house on Saturday morning. It was a picture-perfect day as I drove the ten miles out to Bingham that Saturday morning. There isn't much left in Bingham anymore. I remember when there were about three stores in

Bingham; a man named Lacy Hayes ran a store there for a long time. Now all the stores are gone, and most of the homes are in bad repair.

I don't know when the settlement of Bingham was started, but it would have to have been somewhere in the mid-1800s, because the Reedy Creek Springs began in 1878, and this came to be a rather famous resort in the early 1900s, with a large hotel and cabins that people would come from far and wide to vacation. At that time, there was a railroad that came through Bingham called the Short Line Railroad that ran from Clio to Latta. This is how people came to and from the springs.

Jimmy Berry told me of a cotton gin that his grandfather operated and a lumber mill that was in Bingham. There was also once a post office there. Like a lot of local communities, Bingham was a prosperous little community in that day. I also found out that what we know as Highway 34 was some distance to the south of what is now Highway 34, which of course was dirt at that time. I also learned that a Dr. McSwain, who was the grandfather of local farmer Curt McSwain, had a rather large mercantile store on the old road that is now on the Berry property, and the building is still standing. This building has to be old, because it is made with wooden pegs; there are no nails in this building. Jimmy Berry said he would never tear this building down; he would leave it standing as long as it will. As I passed through Bingham, which by the way is referred to by many local folks as "Bangham," I went about a mile and turned on a dirt road that led me to the Berry property.

I met Chad Garris at the Berry homeplace where Chad now lives. We had never met, but I was impressed with the young man right away. I have always considered myself a pretty good judge of human character, and I could tell from the start that Chad was a straight shooter with a very good head on his shoulders.

Chad moved here from Florence about twelve years ago for the good hunting in this area. He leases the hunting rights on the land owned by Henry Davis, who owns the land adjoining the Berry Farm. Mr. Davis lives in Garden City Beach, South Carolina, and I recently had a very good conversation him. The farm land is rented by Kenneth Long, whose family has worked this land for a very long time.

Chad and I talked for awhile and he asked if I was ready to go to the site of the Bingham Light. I told him I was ready, so we got in Chad's truck and headed down a small dirt road behind his house. Before we left, he showed me a map of the property, and the area where the light is sighted is actually bounded by three properties, the Berry Farm, the Davis Farm and a parcel that is leased by a hunting club run by some Miller guys from Lake View.

Not very far from where we started, Chad turned left onto another dirt road that wound around the edge of the Berry Farm. After traveling for what seemed like a couple of miles, Chad turned up in the area of a small pond. He said we would walk from here. I could tell that he knew exactly where he was going. We crossed a barbed wire fence and some pretty tough briars, and soon we came out on a cornfield that was freshly cut.

As we walked along the edge of the field, I saw discarded shotgun shells. Chad said that this is where some fellows had been dove hunting. I don't know exactly how far we walked, but we came to the old railroad bed, where the rail tracks once lay. We walked along the railroad bed and Chad pointed out that this area was usually covered by water on both sides, but due to the extreme weather this year, it was completely dry. We saw some brick steps where the train used to stop for water and where people would get off the train to get to the Reedy Creek Springs some one hundred years ago. Chad said it was his belief that they would be picked up by wagons that would come from the springs. I cannot find out whether there was ever a depot in Bingham, but I was told there was a ticket office there.

About fifty yards from the site where the light appears, a flock of wild turkeys flew up—I would guess about ten or twelve. Chad said, "The turkeys must not believe in ghosts." Just before we got to the small creek, which is part of Reedy Creek, Chad spied a couple of ducks; this area seemed to be full of wildlife. Chad said the creek was as low as he had ever seen it.

He turned to me and said, "Well, this is the home of the famous Bingham Light." Chad is a no-nonsense fellow, and he said he had seen the light many times and had taken other people to see the mysterious light. He said that in the winter time when the leaves have shed, the light has a different appearance than in the summer when the trees are full of leaves. He said that many people, as well as some experts, had investigated the strange light, and some have concluded that it was swamp gas.

Chad gave me his opinion of the light. He said to me, "I want you to look down this railroad bed which runs into Butler Road to Highway 34." Butler Road was the former railroad, and I could see all the way to Highway 34. He said that at night, you could see the car lights on 34 as they passed by, as well as the red taillights after the headlights passed by. There are several ways of getting to the scene, but Butler Road is the most used. Some of the entrances, such as at the Miller Hunting Club, have been shut off with a gate. Since that has happened, the light has not been seen as much. Chad is persuaded that the light is a reflection of car lights.

It was in the middle of hunting season when Chad took me to the scene of the Bingham Light and he told me that if I would come back after hunting

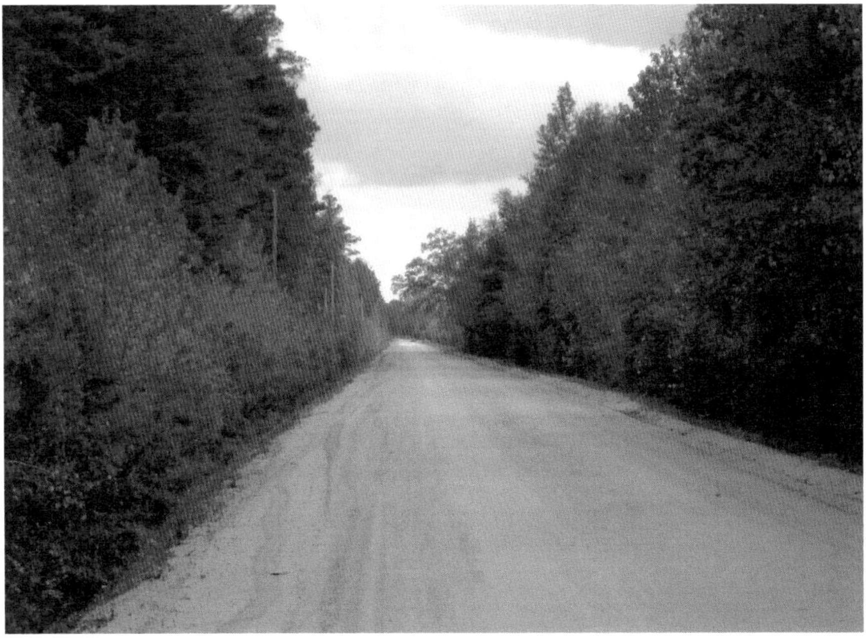

Butler Road leading to the Bingham light location. *Photo by Helen L. Wiggins.*

season that I might get to view the light and decide for myself just what it might be. He did mention that the light was not seen as much lately and that it might take several trips to be seen.

Since beginning this series on the Bingham Light, I have found out a lot concerning this tale that has been passed around for many years. Since the first part of the article came out in the paper, I have heard from many, many people concerning their experiences with the light. As I have already stated, I have not personally seen this mysterious light, but from the stories I have heard and the different types of people I have heard them from, I am persuaded that there is such a light. I still don't have an answer as to what causes the light or where it comes from, but then I don't think anyone else does, either.

I have heard from people of different age groups, ethnic backgrounds and people of different races, and I would say that the greatest majority that I have talked to would be credible people, so I have to take them at their word. When talking to these folks, I ask questions that would lead me to believe that they are telling the truth about what they know and have seen.

I had planned for this to be a rather short chapter, but I may have to stretch it a little further, because I want you to read some of these stories and decide for yourself about these phenomena. There is no way that I can tell them all, but I will tell you about some of the most unusual.

The first article I wrote came out on a Thursday, and that Friday morning I received a call from a Mrs. Georgia McMillan. Mrs. McMillan said she lived on South Butler Road as a child and was then fifty-seven years old. She still lives in the Bingham area, and she still has vivid memories of the light. If you recall, I told you that Butler Road was the old railroad track that has been gone for a very long time.

Mrs. McMillan said that she and her brothers and sisters had seen the light on Butler Road, and not back up in the swamp as many have reported. She said that the light would light up the road at times and would come almost to Highway 34, but there is a small church located about maybe half a mile down the road called Mount Olive Missionary Baptist Church, which started back in the late 1800s from what I can gather.

She stated that the light seemed not to be able to pass this church. She seemed to think the church might in some way have spiritual powers that held the light at bay. She added that the light would usually appear about 10:00 p.m. She also mentioned that at times they thought they would hear the roar of a train, but there was no train.

Today I rode back out to Bingham and went down Butler Road and sure enough, there was the little white church that she had mentioned. Strangely enough, that is the last building on Butler Road.

I received an email from Brian Williams, who lives in the Hamer area and works in maintenance at the Perdue chicken plant. We talked on the phone

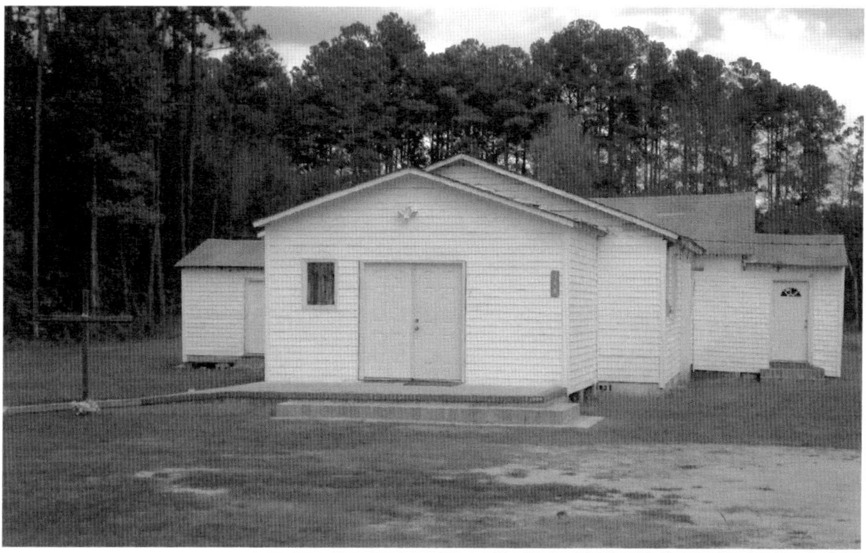

Mount Olive Missionary Baptist Church. *Photo by Helen L. Wiggins.*

for a while, and he said he saw the light about 1996. Brian is thirty-two years old. He said that he and some friends had heard so much about the light that they decided to drive out to Bingham one night and see if they could see the light. He said they turned on Butler Road and went a short ways, and the light appeared just a few yards from where they were. He said this was just past dark, maybe about 8:00 p.m., and the light was right in the middle of the road. It reminded him of a train stopped on a railroad track.

They slowly moved toward the light and it began to move away from them. He said when they got to the end of the road, the light disappeared. They decided to turn around and head back to Highway 34, because they had seen what they came to see. After heading back down Butler Road, someone shouted "It's behind us!" They turned around, and once again the light started moving away. This time he said it changed to a reddish color. When they followed it to the end of Butler Road, it disappeared again. Brian said that this was the only time he went searching for the light, but he says that it was not a car light, and to this day he has no idea what it was.

Derrick Lattymer, a fellow who works with me, approached me and said, "I hear you are writing about the Bingham Light." I asked him if he had seen the light, and he replied, "Many times." Derrick lives just a short distance from Bingham, and he said that he saw the light for the first time when he was five years old. He said it was a big event for them to go searching for the light. He said he never knew of the light hurting or harming anyone. He said he always looked forward to them loading up the family and going to search for the light.

One of the most interesting stories about the light came from Suzanne Alford, who now lives in Latta and is sixty-one years of age. She said they moved to Bingham in 1966 from the same farm where I was born and reared on. Her mother was Alafarir McCants, who was born in 1900, and joined the Mount Olive Church in 1910, so this church must go back to the 1800s. Suzanne said her mother told her that the story of the Bingham Light came about from a man named Wylam Wynn, whose wife was named Rhee. Neither Suzanne nor I am sure about the spelling of the names—this is a story that was handed down from her mother.

It seems that Mr. Wynn worked for the railroad, and when the train stopped for water very near where the light is most commonly seen, it was his job to pump water into the train engine. Well, the story goes that it was Mr. Wynn who lost his head on the railroad track and he is the one still looking for his head. Suzanne said she had seen the light more times than she could count, and had seen it in many places. She said that she had picked cotton on the farmland that borders the swamp where the light appears. I mentioned that Chad Garris and I parked at a small pond to get to the location of the light and Suzanne said that while picking cotton at dusk she had seen the light rise out of that pond. She also mentioned that she had seen the light come up out of the ditch that runs alongside Butler Road. She also believes that the church has some hold over the light; she says she has never seen the light past the church. Well, folks, are you thoroughly confused by now? I can tell you that I certainly am confused to the point that I want to see this light for myself, and when hunting season is over, I plan to search for the "Bingham Light."

I don't know much more than when I started about this light that has mystified so many people, and there are so many unanswered questions that I would like to know, but it has been most intriguing to hear what people have shared with me. One thing I have tried to find out is when the light first began to appear. I have asked countless people this question and nobody seems to really know, as well as a lot of other things connected with the light.

The best answer I can come up with is from a lady who says that she has seen the light for many years, and she said that it first appeared to her in 1958. The light as I have mentioned began to get popular in the 1980s and has probably drawn hundreds of people, if not thousands, to view this strange thing, whatever it might be.

One thing that mystifies me is that the light does not appear to all people. I talked to a lady this week that lives near the area, and she said she had searched for the light maybe twenty times and had yet to see it, so she just gave up. I have talked to several people who have told me the same thing. They said they would go with people who had seen the light, but it would not appear while they were there. My question is: does it only appear to certain people?

From what I can gather, people have come from all over the state and some from out of state in search of the light. As I have mentioned, a lot of folks talk about certain houses and cemeteries that they are persuaded to believe are haunted. They talk about certain sounds and feelings they have had in these places. There are people who study and deal in the paranormal; they have machines and gadgets that are supposed to record strange sounds and events to prove that a certain place might be haunted.

There was a pretty big article in the *Florence Morning News* this week about a group of people who go around seeking out ghosts and things that are abnormal. One of these people is supposed to be a physic and is said to have had communication with the dead. I have heard people say that they were visited by a former friend or relative that has passed on and actually talked to them. Well, I have my ideas of such a thing, and I call it "hogwash." I seem to be a person who dreams a lot, and I have had many dreams of the dead, including my mother and father as well as many other folks that have departed this life. There have been times that I have woken from sleep during these dreams and would be disturbed somewhat, but there was no one in my room, so I usually just go back to sleep.

Before we get back to the "Bingham Light," I would like to mention a cemetery located in the Mechanicsville area of Darlington County called Montrose Cemetery that many of these folks who deal in the paranormal say is haunted for sure. I wouldn't know, because I believe cemeteries are sacred and hallowed places, and I don't think we have any business roaming around cemeteries at night trying to hear strange things.

Getting back to the "Bingham Light," lights seem to be a pretty common thing in different areas around the country. I was told of a Mr. Carl Ivey who supposedly had a lot of information on the light. He lives in Saint Paul's, North Carolina, so I called him one night, and as soon as we began to talk, he said that he didn't know anything about the Bingham Light, and that the light he was familiar with was a light that would appear in the area around Delco, North Carolina—a little place on Highway 74, about eighteen miles from Wilmington.

He said that before the highway was made four lanes to Wilmington that this strange light (looking much like a lantern light) would appear over in a swampy area off the highway. He stated that he and his wife had seen this light many times, and it also had a story of a railroad that went with it. He said that this was a very old tale that went back to the 1800s. Mr. Ivey said that in the late 1970s, when Highway 74 was made four lanes, a great deal of the swamp had to be filled in. Since the completion of the highway, the light has never been seen again, so was it really swamp gas? Or did the light just decide to move away?

I'm not sure if all of you know or not, but the final path of the new Interstate I-73 will come right through Bingham, and—you got it—right through the home of the "Bingham Light." I understand there will also be an interchange in Bingham. Will this mean the end of the light? Or will thousands of tourists see this strange light as they pass through? Will we finally find out if the "Bingham Light" is fact or fiction? I cannot ignore the many stories that have been told to me about the light. I believe most of these people to be credible. I believe they saw something, but what did they see?

This old storyteller will probably not be around when I-73 is completed, but some of you younger folks may one day know the reason for the "Bingham Light," or then maybe you won't. Only time will tell. After writing this, we received an email from Jeff Dudley, a well-respected man in Marlboro County, about his experience seeing the light. Also Eddie Dial, who saw the light, came by with a good story. Space has run out, but I wanted to recognize them. We are hoping Jeff will publish a book in the near future about Marlboro County, as he is well qualified to do so.

"CROSS ROADS" HENRY BERRY

Just a few miles outside of Latta on Highway 38 West is a place called Berry's Cross Roads. I guess I have passed by there a hundred times, but never really knew where it got its name until I started researching some family history about a year ago.

One of the first Berrys that we find in this part of the country was a man named Andrew Berry, who settled at Sandy Bluff on the Great Pee Dee River in the Marion District (now Marion County) about 1736. It was said that Andrew Berry was a man small in stature, who married—but his wife is unknown to me—and the couple had ten children: six sons and four daughters.

Two of his sons were Henry and Stephen. The Henry listed here is not the "Cross Roads" Henry Berry, but was an uncle of "Cross Roads." The uncle was said to be an intelligent man for that day and time. He served as justice of the peace for several years. I have seen his signature on some very old documents. He married a Miss Hays, and had land granted to him in 1786 on Little Reedy Creek. He accumulated a good bit of property in his lifetime. It was also said that he donated the land where Catfish Creek Baptist Church now stands. The church was organized in 1802, but it is believed the church may have been started as early as 1750 in another location. This has not been documented that I can find.

The first Henry Berry lived to be over ninety years old and died in 1853. If you recall, this Henry had a brother named Stephen, wife unknown, who also had a considerable family, but only two sons, Henry (later known as "Cross Roads") and Andrew Stephen Berry. Born in 1796, Henry Berry was the grandson of old Andrew Berry. Henry married Miss Charity Crawford.

Legend has it that Miss Crawford was betrothed to another man by her parents, but she loved Henry Berry and one night slipped out her bedroom window with Henry Berry and became his wife. They settled on 150 acres of land at what is now known as Berry's Cross Roads.

The Crawford family was well-to-do, but that family has gone from this part of the country. So Henry and his wife started their married life on 150 acres of undeveloped land. He had very little means, but it was said that he was a man of good business sense—honest and upright in his business dealings. He applied himself strictly to his business of farming. At first he acquired land slowly but surely. He took care of what he had and did not try to make a fast dollar. He did nothing for show or ostentation at county or state fairs. He lived well, but without wastefulness. He stayed away from debt throughout his entire life. Henry Berry worked to make a profit with his land. He acquired an estate of over 10,000 acres in his lifetime.

Henry Berry raised eight children: five sons and three daughters. Most of his property was deeded to his children before his death. This is where the name Berry's Cross Roads came from, named after the man who was known as "Cross Roads" Henry Berry.

Henry was a successful farmer, having accumulated a good estate. He managed his money well and made good business decisions during his lifetime. He was known to be a man of honesty and integrity, a man who got along well with everybody in the community. Henry Berry lived a long life, born January 13, 1796, and died July 9, 1876.

The rest of the story is about how his funeral was carried out. About fifteen years before his death, Mr. Berry was plowing in his fields and he had the occasion to take up the bodies of two dead children, and when he saw their condition, he vowed that his body would be burned and not buried.

Of course, this was before the days of embalming and steel vaults. Cremation as we know it was not thought of. So Henry Berry set out to plan the way his body would be disposed of. He went into the woods and selected certain lightwood trees that would be used in the burning of his body. He also selected the exact place that his body was to be burned. He discussed the matter with his family, and his children were astonished. They tried their best to talk him out of such a thing, but Henry Berry said his mind was made up, and those who did not honor his wishes would be disinherited. He inserted into his will that if his wishes were not carried out, all his fortune would go to his church.

The old gentleman took sick and lingered for several months; Henry Berry departed this life on Sunday, July 9, 1876.

The funeral service at the church where he was once a member was held, and an appropriate discourse was delivered at his home on Monday night by the Reverend J.P. Lide, a prominent Marion Baptist minister.

Early next morning, his body, encased in a wooden coffin lined inside and out with black velvet, was carried on a mule-drawn cart to the place

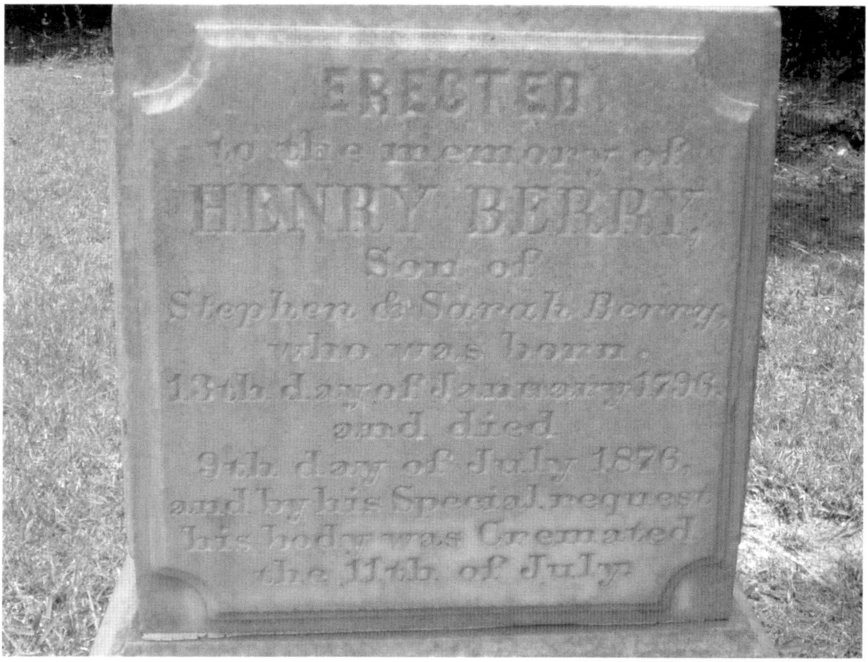

Henry Berry Memorial information. *Photo by Helen L. Wiggins.*

that he had specified. At this place, three lightwood logs, each two feet in diameter, were placed on the ground and the coffin deposited on the logs. Then sufficient lightwood was placed on the logs and around the coffin, until the coffin was hidden from view. It was said the stack reached eight feet in height. Henry Berry had contracted with a man named William Hurling before his death to oversee the burning of his body for a fee of $500.

Several male members of the old man's family were present. It was said that about one hundred people were in attendance. Torches were lit on all four sides at one time and in just a few minutes, the raging fire resembled a large building burning. The thick black smoke rose over one hundred feet into the air. It was Mr. Berry's wishes that his remains be completely consumed until his ashes mingled into the soil. When the fire went out, this had not been achieved, so the fire was restarted. It took six hours to complete the burning of Mr. Berry's body.

In a story told to Mrs. Lucy Sellers in April 1945, Mr. Henry Hays, who was ninety-four at that time, said that he was at the funeral and cremation of Henry Berry.

Today, cremations are a common thing. There are several crematories in the area where a person can have their bodies sent to be cremated if

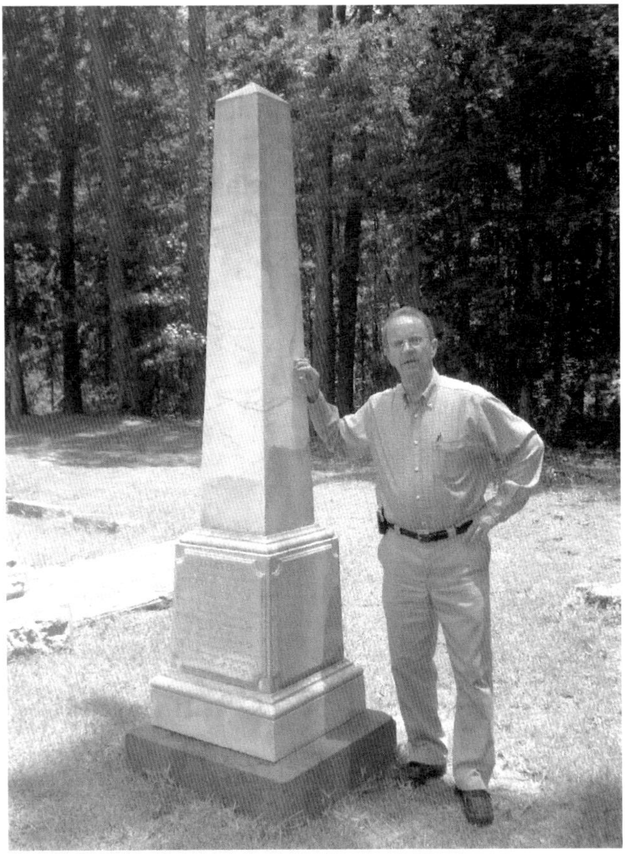

Henry Berry Monument and author. *Courtesy of Helen L. Wiggins.*

they desire. I had a good friend in Florence, South Carolina, who chose to be cremated. It is believed that on July 11, 1876, "Cross Roads" Henry Berry could have been the first person in the state of South Carolina to be cremated. There stands today a memorial very near Berry's Cross Roads in the Union Cemetery, Latta, Dillon County, to honor the late "Cross Roads" Henry Berry.

THE ALLIGATOR HOLE

I am sure that everybody has certain places or things that stand out in their minds from their childhood that they have fond memories of. I would like to share with you a place that I remember from my childhood.

I was born and reared about seven miles from the Free States community in Dillon County, South Carolina, off Highway 34, just past what was known as Walker Bethea's store. There were not a lot of places to go back then in the early 1950s, except when we would visit relatives or go to Dillon maybe once a week. As a country boy, when you were not working on the farm, you found the best way you could to entertain yourself.

I have always loved to fish, and the closest place for me to go fishing was a small creek called Reedy Creek about a mile and a half from where I lived. There is a bridge that crosses over the creek that we referred to as the "white bridge." In the spring and summer, folks would get their fishing poles and dig up some earthworms and head to the white bridge.

Now, there was not a great deal of fish to be caught in the creek, mostly a few catfish, or some small bream or perch. Where the bridge was located, the creek was probably not over twenty five feet wide, and I don't think it was over five feet deep in any place.

I remember an African American man named Jake Pierce that would sit in the same place under the bridge on a stump and would usually catch enough catfish in a day to make himself a catfish stew. Jake was a man that loved to laugh, and every time he would catch a fish, you could hear him laughing for half a mile.

The most plentiful fish in the creek was what we called "red fin pike." The pike was a slender fish about six to eight inches in length, and had a red fin on the bottom of the fish. Now it was seldom that the pike would bite a hook while still fishing; you had to "jigger" for them. The way you would do this was to bait your hook with a small piece of "fatback" and tie a piece of red cloth to the bait. You would take your cane pole with about a four- or five-foot line and let the bait sink a foot or so under the water and drag the bait in a jerky motion along under the water. The pike could not resist the bait, and usually you would have one on the hook. After you caught the first fish, you would cut the red fin off the fish's belly, allowing a good portion of the meat to stay with the fin, and that is what you would use as bait until it was gone. After I learned the technique, I would usually come home with a pretty good catch of fish. The pike was a tasty fish; my mother would dress them and fry them crisp in a cornmeal batter. When the fish were cooked, you could peel the backbone out and eat the rest.

About two miles up the creek was a wide place in the creek that turned into a lake. This was referred to as the "Alligator Hole." This place was located almost behind the home of Sue and the late Bobby McLaurin, about a mile over in the woods. The Alligator Hole had a lot of myths and tales told about it. Some of the older folks would tell about staying away from there because it was full of alligators and "lamp eels." For you who never heard of a lamp eel, it was supposedly an eel with legs that would kill you with one bite. Also there was supposed to be a lot of "coach whips" around this part of the woods. I have heard many tales about coach whips growing up. The coach whip was supposed to be a long black snake with a forked tail. It was said that when a coach whip would get after you, he would catch his tail in his mouth and roll like a wheel, and there was no way you could outrun him. He was supposed to be very deadly.

As a boy of about ten or eleven, I believed these stories, and I never thought about trying to find the Alligator Hole, but as time went by I got a little braver, and thought about going to find it. There was a McDowell family that lived not too far from the creek. Mr. and Mrs. Boyd McDowell had five sons, all of whom were older than me except the youngest boy, Donald, who today lives in Georgia. Donald is the only surviving son, and I saw him last year at his brother George's funeral for the first time in forty years. I was at their house one day, and the boys that were home said they were going fishing, and asked if I wanted to go. I told them I didn't have my fishing pole. They said that was all right, that I would not need a pole, and they pulled out this net that looked to be about six or eight feet wide. I asked where they were going, and they said to the Alligator Hole.

Well, I got a little weak in the knees—these fellows were talking about going to one of the most dangerous places on earth in my mind. They could tell that I was a little afraid, but the older boys assured me they would take care of me. So, off we went across the field and into the woods to the dreaded Alligator Hole. A couple of the boys had "foot tubs," and some of you city folks might not know what a foot tub is, but it is about half the size of a wash tub.

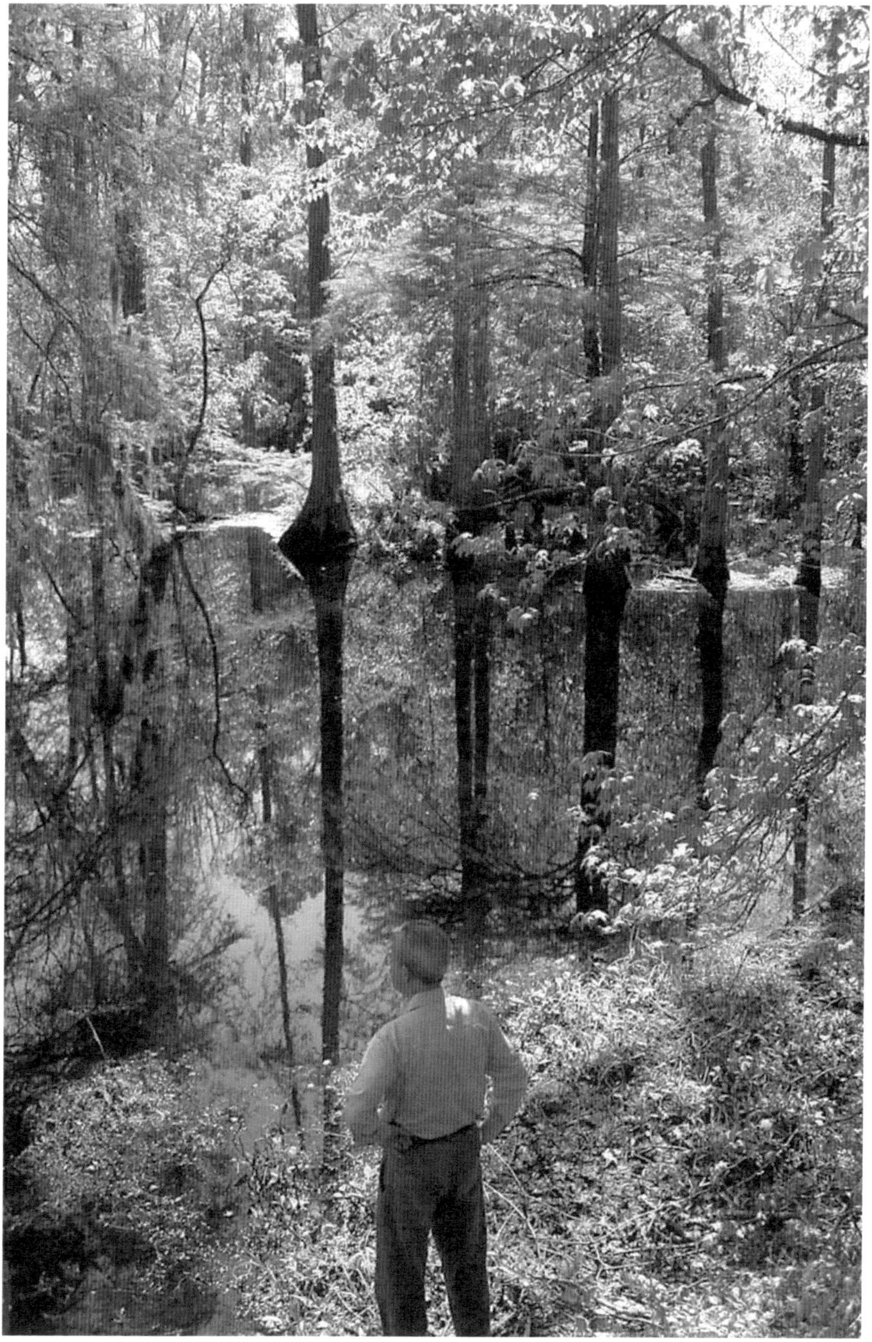

Author near the Alligator Hole. *Photo by Helen L. Wiggins.*

After walking for what seemed like an hour, we arrived at the Alligator Hole. I don't guess it was over forty feet wide, but it looked big to me. All I could think about were the alligators, lamp eels and coach whips. They sat down and began to pull off their shoes and roll up their pants legs. These fools were actually going to get into this water.

They told me to do the same thing, and by this time I was petrified, but some of these guys were eighteen to twenty years old, so I put my trust in them. Two of them took the net out in the water, and held it by the wooden handles that were on each end. They told the rest of us to go down the creek about twenty five feet and take the hoes that we had brought and splash the water with them, which would run the fish toward the net.

Well, I got into the water, but was careful to stay pretty close to the bank. We began to make noise and push the hoes along under the water toward the net. Things began to hit me on the legs, and I didn't want to imagine what they might be. The closer we got to the net, I could see that the guys holding the net were straining and one said "Boys, we have got a real catch here." One of the boys said to come and help pull up the net. When we got the net out of the water and on the bank, I had never seen so many fish in my life. We filled the two foot tubs that we had brought with red fin pike with only one pull of the net. By that time, I had forgotten all about the "critters" that we were supposed to run into.

After that I went to the Alligator Hole many times. I remember on one trip there was an African American guy with us, whose name has escaped me, but when we pulled the net he said, "O Lord, there is a lamp eel." Well, I saw what he was talking about, which looked like a long lizard with short legs. I believe they are called salamanders, and are completely harmless. I never saw any alligators, and have never been able to find anything about lamp eels or coach whips.

My wife and I took a trip over to the creek to take some pictures. While we were there, a man named Samuel Watson, who lives in the community, stopped by, and we talked about fishing in years gone by at Reedy Creek. We talked about the Alligator Hole and he said to me, "Mister, there are things in that swamp you won't find in books." Who knows? Maybe he is right.

A lot of timber has been cut in the swamp, and the beavers have made so many dams that the main stream of the creek has been rerouted. I don't guess anybody fishes there anymore, but I have fond memories of that old place when I was growing up.

ABOUT THE AUTHOR

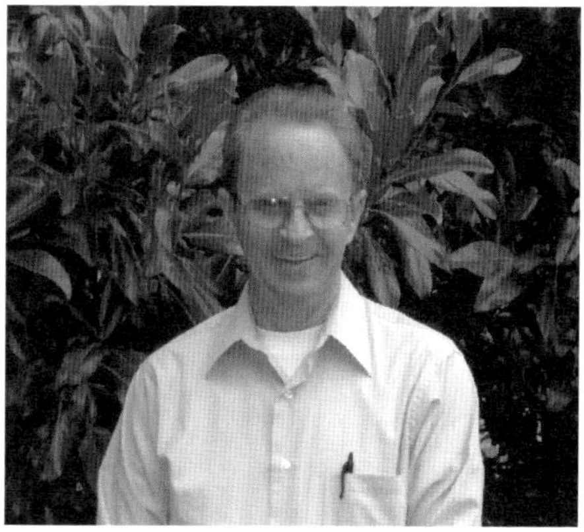

In August of 2003, Carley Wiggins decided to write an article for the local newspaper called "A Dying Breed." This was a story of a small country store that was closing after twenty-two years of service to the community in which it was located. As far as he knew, this would be the first and only newspaper article he would ever write.

When the article was published, the response from readers was staggering. Many people called and made personal contact, asking Mr. Wiggins to write more. The editor of the paper said they would be glad to publish future articles. At the age of sixty-two, Carley Wiggins found a new talent and a new career as a freelance writer.

Five years later, he has written over 250 articles. Many of these articles are in series form, with some as long as twenty weeks. Wiggins has written about a little of everything, focusing on little-heard-of places and people in the Pee Dee area. Carley Wiggins has won four major awards for articles he has written, and is nominated for a fifth for 2008. For a man that has never considered himself a writer, but instead just a simple storyteller, he has heard from people all over the United States and several foreign countries.

It is from the encouragement of his readers that he decided to put some of his more popular articles in book form so that his followers can have this permanent record, here called *Remembering Dillon County, South Carolina.*